TRADITION AND CHANGE

Harold T. Shapiro became the tenth president of the University of Michigan in January, 1980, and will become the eighteenth president of Princeton University in January, 1988. He is a graduate of McGill University, holds a doctorate in economics from Princeton University, and has been a professor of economics and public policy at the University of Michigan since 1964. His numerous scholarly publications reflect his interests in econometrics and public policy, and he is best known for his influential work in the area of economic forecasting. For fourteen years he codirected the University of Michigan's nationally respected economic forecasting operation, the Research Seminar in Quantitative Economics.

Dr. Shapiro's stature as a national leader in higher education was most recently recognized by his election to the chairmanship of the Association of American Universities for 1987–88. He has also been extensively involved in government, foundation, and corporate activities, where his service includes membership on the Council of Government-University-Industry Research Roundtable; the Governor's High Technology Task Force for the State of Michigan; the Board of Trustees of the Alfred P. Sloan Foundation; and the boards of directors of Dow Chemical Corporation, Kellogg Company, and Unisys Corporation.

He is married to Vivian B. Shapiro, a scholar, teacher, and clinician in the field of infant mental health, and is the father of four grown daughters.

The University of Michigan was privileged to have this extraordinary scholar and leader as its president for the past eight years.

Harold T. Shapiro

TRADITION AND CHANGE

Perspectives on Education and Public Policy

Ann Arbor
The University of Michigan Press

Some of the essays in this volume are adapted from or incorporate parts of previously published articles. "Inflation: The Social and Political Challenge" incorporates portions of an article in *Dividend*, Fall 1980. "U.S. Productivity Growth: A 'Growing' Concern" is from an article in the *Michigan Technic*, Spring 1982. "Michigan Can Manufacture a Solid Future" is from an article in the *Detroit Free Press*, January 9, 1986. "The National Research Effort: Funding and Policy Issues" incorporates portions of articles in *Issues in Science and Technology* 2, no. 3 (Spring 1986) and the *New York Times*, April 15, 1984. "Paradox, Change, and Choice: An Economist's View of Some Current Health Care Resource Issues" is from an article in the *American Journal of Cardiology* 56 (1985). "Openness in an Academic Community" incorporates portions of an article in *Science*, July 6, 1984.

For my wife, Vivian
Scholar, teacher, clinician, advisor, and critic
Her voice is everywhere in these words.

Preface

This collection of essays is based upon speeches and papers written during the eight years I had the privilege of serving as president of the University of Michigan. Some are close to their original form; others have been significantly modified to avoid repetition and to focus on the principal themes that have been the subject of my interest and attention. I have gathered these essays together as a way of saying thank you to the many supporters of the University of Michigan who have helped to make my years as president the most exciting and rewarding experience of my career.

These have been eventful years at the University of Michigan. They have been a time of extraordinary challenges and important new accomplishments for the university. Not everything has turned out the way we hoped, but many achievements exceeded our expectations, and the world of higher education continues to recognize the University of Michigan as one of the most distinguished research universities in the world. Everyone who has participated in these exciting developments will, I hope, share my satisfaction at having served a great institution and carried on a great tradition.

Many, both within and beyond the academic community, have worked tirelessly with me on behalf of the university. Our motivations for these dedicated efforts have included: gratitude for past experiences at the University of Michigan; a wish to serve our state or country; and the desire to play a role in encouraging new directions in science, in the performing and creative arts, and in our understanding of society. Most of all, however, we have been committed to supporting the aspirations and human potential of current and future generations of students, teachers, and scholars.

During my tenure as president, I have had occasion to reflect on a variety of issues that related, directly or indirectly, to the University of Michigan and its many commitments. These essays offer a representative sample of my thinking on some of these issues. I share them with you now as you shared your own efforts with Vivian and me, as we all worked together to secure the future of the University of Michigan.

Vivian and I are now moving to a new set of challenges, but we shall always have a special place in our hearts for this university and especially for the many wonderful people associated with it. We will always find ways to continue our involvement in supporting the future of the University of Michigan.

A number of colleagues played a significant role in helping me assemble these essays. My assistants, first Susan S. Lipschutz and then Robin M. Jacoby, provided thoughtful advice as the essays were originally written. Margaret A. Lourie expertly edited all of the essays in the preparation of this volume. My wife Vivian—a teacher, scholar, and clinician in her own right—has always been my toughest, most honest, and most helpful critic and advisor. Many of these essays reflect ideas we developed together. Finally, I want to thank all my colleagues whose thoughtful criticism has improved—and perhaps redeemed—my own efforts.

Harold T. Shapiro
Ann Arbor, Michigan
December, 1987

Contents

The State and National Economies

Inflation: The Social and Political Challenge   *3*

U.S. Productivity Growth: A "Growing" Concern   *10*

Michigan Can Manufacture a Solid Future   *15*

The Economic Program of the Reagan Administration   *18*

Implications of Changing Technologies

Public Policy and the International Transfer of Technology   *27*

The National Research Effort: Funding and Policy Issues   *41*

Information Networking   *47*

The Importance of the Humanities in a Technological Age   *51*

Policy and Resource Issues in a Contemporary Democracy

Confronting Reality and Building the Future: Race Relations and
the Future of Our Liberal Democracy   *63*

Are Schools for Learning?   *72*

Philanthropy: Tradition and Change   *80*

Paradox, Change, and Choice: An Economist's View of Some
Current Health Care Resource Issues   *86*

The Federal Role in U.S. Higher Education   *100*

The Organization and Management of the University

Critic and Servant: The Role of the University   *111*

American Higher Education: A Special Tradition Faces a Special
Challenge   *118*

The Modern Research University   *132*

Managing Research Institutions under Resource
Constraints   *139*

The Future of the Kaleidoscope: Medical Education and the
University   *149*

Values in Higher Education

The National Debate on Higher Education   *163*
Openness in an Academic Community   *172*
The Nature, Function, and Future of Academic Tenure   *182*
Excellence and Equity   *190*

The State and
National Economies

Inflation: The Social and Political Challenge

For the first time since the Great Depression, Americans increasingly lack confidence in the capacity of our economic system to deal effectively with its multiple responsibilities. The era of naive and unrealistic expectations, so seductive to us for a time, seems to be over. We are apprehensive that we will not be able to develop solutions to our lagging productivity, our continuing inflation, our energy "problem," or a host of other "economic" issues currently on the national agenda—issues such as unemployment (particularly of young people and minorities), environmental decay, economic security, trade policy, and the role of government in "guiding" our economic destiny.

Our present uneasiness regarding the economy may partake in a broader current in contemporary social thought that calls into question the whole idea of economic progress, an idea that has undergirded our economic self-consciousness since the founding of the republic. On the other hand, our increasing economic anxiety may arise from the decline of U.S. dominance in world affairs. From the end of World War II until quite recently, the United States was *the* major force in world economic, military, political, cultural, and scientific activities. Now, however, the economies of our chief trading partners are, by and large, growing faster than our own, we have become reliant on foreign capital, and the cultural expressions of other societies increasingly share the stage with our own.

Yet despite our current difficulties, the U.S. economy has never grown faster, on the average, than in the decades since the Great Depression. Further, the years since World War II have witnessed a greater stability in real output and unemployment than at any other time in our history. The desire to return to an earlier economic "utopia," then, is mostly misinformed.

The post–World War II economy, however, has also exhibited a much greater tendency to persistent and chronic inflation than ever before, and I will be exploring the causes of this troubling tendency in the remainder of this essay. Inflation is of concern because of the capricious changes in the distribution of revenue it causes, because it discourages traditional forms of savings and investment, because it increases the tax burden and makes all types of economic planning and decision making more difficult. As a subject of inquiry, inflation like religion is both old and new, both clear and mysterious. It has been extensively studied since ancient times (since money was invented), but it seems to remain—with its mysteries intact—near the top of our list of economic concerns and puzzles.

Clearly some new forces are both causing our economy to be more inflation prone and making it more difficult (i.e., more costly) to "unwind" a persistent inflation once it gets underway. These forces, I believe, have more to do with the response of our political system to our changing social agenda than with any fundamental changes in our economic system itself. Thus the problem is, at its heart, not simply economic, but political and social as well.

It is clear that a persistent inflation can only be sustained in an economic environment of continual federal budget deficits, financed in part through monetary expansion. But it is only at a symptomatic level that the phenomenon of inflation is a matter of "too much money chasing too few goods." Nor can our continuing inflation be fully blamed on OPEC oil prices, harvest failures, domestic oil cartels, labor unions, or new developments in the international monetary system. These factors have their impact to be sure, but their effect is, by and large, relatively short-lived, and they cannot adequately explain a sustained inflation of half a decade or longer.

To understand the underlying causes of inflation, we must ask *why* our government has continually, through Democratic and Republican administrations alike, made the *political* choice of running large budgetary deficits and financing them, in part, by increasing the supply of money.[1] To put the matter more directly, economic policies are forged in the furnace of national politics. The goals of governmental economic policy are selected within a political process that balances the economic, social, and political interests of different constituencies against one another.

Inflationary policies are not, I suggest, thrust upon society by an unknowing government or an inadequate Federal Reserve Board.

Rather, these policies represent the response of government to the political pressure exerted by constituents who want ever-increasing benefits from the federal government without commensurate tax increases and/or a staunch defense of their share of the national income. They also represent the desire of legislators and other officials to avoid the short-run economic, social, and political dislocation costs of increased unemployment and decreased output that might follow in the wake of a less inflationary policy.

To understand how we have arrived at this state of affairs, it is important to appreciate the tradition of national agenda setting in the United States and some of the critical changes that have taken place in this mechanism since the end of World War II. Historically, the genius of American democracy was that it did not take a simplistic view of our heterogeneous cultural environment. It did not proclaim the authority of a single morality. Rather, it put into place a set of integrative institutions that could establish a social order, designate the necessary leadership, and provide, through certain idealized conceptions of freedom of contract and equal opportunity, for the sharing of our national resources. Most importantly, however, these integrative processes were governed by the art of compromise and mutual reconciliation of our diverse interests. Throughout our history, as our society has changed, diverse groups have sought differing and often mutually exclusive responses. The capacity of our integrative institutions to develop compromises and our willingness to accept such compromises account for the long and relatively peaceful history of our domestic polity.

The ideology that justified and the political process that enforced these various processes never took seriously the quick elimination of all injustices and inequalities. A much more difficult aspiration was involved—one that simultaneously reflected both our diversity and our homogeneity. We seemed to understand that equality and injustice had many complex dimensions and that our attention should focus only on the most offensive inequalities and on the decentralization of power. We knew that, in a complex and dynamic world, if we were to avoid tyranny—including the tyranny of the state—we would have to support processes of mutual reconciliation. Such a social order has little tolerance for groups whose views admit of no compromise.

After 1945, however, this traditional social order began to

change. The United States emerged from World War II with a national legacy based on the combined experiences of the war and the Great Depression. From the Depression came a new national sensitivity to the economic and cultural distress of the unemployed, the working poor, the elderly, and the special burdens that had been placed on particular minority groups. The experience of the war added to this new sensitivity the notion that we not only should but could and would rectify this undesirable situation.

We determined that the federal government, particularly federal transfer payment programs, would be our vehicle for achieving these new social aims. Unfortunately, we did not succeed in deciding just who would provide the tax revenues necessary to support these additional government responsibilities. At times, economic growth took care of this financing problem, but in the end the seeds of our recent inflationary experiences were sown by this transformation of the federal government's role and our inability to decide how to finance it.

Thus began a long procession of special (and often worthy) interest groups asking the federal government to protect (guarantee?) their economic and other interests. We became an economy of innumerable bargaining blocks, each one of which, no matter how small, learned to use our system to promote its own interest. Consequently, our ability to select and act on national priorities has become impaired. We stall one another's initiatives and seem to have lost much of our essential capacity for meaningful compromise. It is not that we cannot identify solutions to certain national problems but that we will not adopt any solutions that may impose a sacrifice on a particular group.

The solution to any significant national problem will require economic sacrifices from someone. If we are to remain a viable and progressive society, we must have a workable mechanism for deciding the appropriate distribution of such sacrifices. Let me offer some examples. If we want more investment, someone has to do the saving. If we want more productivity, someone has to work more effectively today to lay a better foundation for our future. If we wish to remain an effective military power, we must sacrifice certain other benefits. As for the energy problem, we all believe to some extent in energy independence, but some group objects to every solution that is proposed. As a result we have so far not been able fully to adopt *any* of the possible paths to this goal. Other examples are all around us.

How does this national paralysis relate to the problem of inflation? When the federal government cannot mediate the various demands on the national treasury, it has a short-run, often short-sighted, alternative—financing these options through monetary expansion. When Congress has finally expended all tax revenue and cannot or will not expand the national debt, it can continue to "satisfy" constituents' demands, at least in the short run, by printing money.[2]

Thus, while no group in society explicitly demands more inflation, pressures for the government to pursue a more inflationary policy arise because there are always groups—those next in line for federal support—that benefit from such a policy. That is, at any given moment some groups will believe that financing certain government programs by "printing money" will work very much more to their advantage than either forgoing federal support or being held responsible for tax increases. These groups may be defense contractors, college students, welfare recipients, conservationists, farmers—the list is almost endless.

The persistent inflation of the last decade is, therefore, largely a symptom of our political failure to agree on how to allocate our national resources. It points to a kind of institutional arteriosclerosis within our pluralistic democracy. Our policies have served the genuine interests of certain changing coalitions, but in the long run they have threatened to undermine the institutions that enable us to live together.

Unfortunately, the economics profession has never expended much effort on analyzing the relationship between the political process and economic policy. Economists in general explain the persistent application of "inappropriate" (i.e., inefficient) policies (e.g., tariffs) as the personal failings of those in charge of public policy. The possibility that these policies may be serving the vital interests of those in power or their constituents (i.e., be a rational strategy in an environment of scarcity) is hardly given a second reading. Inflation, especially continuing inflation, *is* a policy and *does* serve perceived group interests, at least in the short run. Only by recognizing this aspect of the issue can we come to a better understanding of the source of continuing inflation and its cure.

At any given moment, the government must balance the pressures for an inflationary budget policy against the benefit of a less inflationary economic policy. That is, our representatives must try to find the appropriate balance or trade-off between the short-run political and economic dislocation costs of an anti-inflationary policy and the adverse effects of a policy leading to a sustained inflation. This balance will be crucially affected by the particular institutional structure within which the economy is embedded. There would, for example, be critical differences in this calculus between the United States and Japan or Germany. This cross-cultural variation stems, in large part, from the basic differences in the organization of the economy's key institutions and from differential participation in the international economic system. In addition, however, the nature of this balance will depend on the complexity of the political negotiations required to ratify an alternative noninflationary solution, such as a tax increase, and on the overall status of the international economic system, in which a single country—no matter how large—is but one participant.

Thus, inflation is embedded in the U.S. economic and political system in a complicated way. It relates not only to such economic acts as the setting of wages and prices and the existing structure of key economic institutions, but also to a wide spectrum of other current socioeconomic considerations. Furthermore, a sustained inflation cannot be overcome at zero cost. As we move to a less inflationary economic environment, there will be unpleasant side effects (e.g., slower growth) in the short run. The costs of these side effects must be balanced against the impact of a continuing, or even accelerating, inflation. Once again, the nature and severity of these side effects will depend on the structure of existing economic institutions and markets. For example, if prices do not respond quickly to fluctuations in aggregate demand (as seems to be increasingly the case in the United States), then moving from a more to a less inflationary policy will require a more difficult adjustment and create harsher side effects. This undoubtedly explains, in part, why the contemporary U.S. economy tends toward a persistent inflation.

In the end, sustained inflation does not work. Its presumable benefits are temporary since they are eliminated in the next round of the wage-price spiral; and meanwhile considerable long-run damage may have been done. The solution, in my opinion, is to encourage public officials to look beyond the immediate pressures facing them and begin to confront the underlying problems and conflicts that create them. Moreover, we, the electorate, must face up to the implications of our own demands.

The major underlying conflict is caused by the claims of different groups in society to what they believe to be their fair share of the national income. Unfortunately, if we add up all these "fair shares," they much more than exhaust the total available. We must, therefore, somehow find a way to mediate society's expectations regarding appropriate efforts, rewards, and sacrifices. We must decide not only how to distribute these efforts and rewards among the current work force but how to measure our own claims against those of future generations. A lot is at stake.

Although the accelerated and persistent inflation in the contemporary U.S. economy largely results from greater monetary expansion, it cannot be explained solely on this basis. Two other factors also enter in: first, and most important, the puzzling slowdown in the growth of labor productivity; second, the series of "supply shocks" (e.g., OPEC oil price increases, harvest failure) that have not only been destabilizing but have made it more difficult to maintain a noninflationary policy. A careful and balanced evaluation of the evidence, however, indicates that it is the financing of government deficits through monetary expansion that will remain the chief cause of persistent inflation.

1. To fully articulate the various ways the government could finance a budget deficit would require a detailed analysis of both the Treasury's operating position and the Federal Reserve's balance sheet. The most important methods of financing a deficit, however, are an increase in government debt held by the public and an increase in "high powered" money. Needless to say, the behavior of the commercial banking sector and the public will also help determine the monetary impact of any sequence of government budget positions.

2. In this context, I use the phrase "printing money" to cover all those actions that lead from a budgetary deficit to an expansion of the money supply.

U.S. Productivity Growth: A "Growing" Concern

Because the U.S. economy has recently been in trouble, considerable national attention has focused on such economic issues as inflation, unemployment, declining productivity, taxes, and government deficits. In such a disquieting environment even "dull" economic statistics have acquired a new urgency. The purpose of this short note is to discuss certain issues surrounding one of these problems: our declining productivity performance.

National productivity growth (the increase in the volume of goods and services produced per unit of work effort) slowed dramatically in the United States during the last decade. The annual productivity growth rate in the private nonfarm business sector, which had been between 2 and 3 percent for several decades, began to drop in the late 1960s and has fallen to extremely low levels since 1973.

Continued weak growth in productivity has profound social as well as economic implications. On the economic side, failure to improve productivity implies a corresponding inability to generate any economic growth or improvement in our standard of living. Compare, for example, real wages in the United States during the 1947–73 period with those of the more recent period. In the years 1947–73 annual gains in real wages mirrored our productivity growth at about 2.5 percent per year. Annual growth in real wages, however, fell to 0.9 percent during the 1973–79 period. During this period families achieved higher standards of living largely by increasing the number of workers in the family rather than through gains in productivity. We have yet to understand the impact of this development on the American family.

Yet anxiety over productivity is not simply a materialistic concern for economic growth or jobs and job development. On the social side, poor productivity performance would, for example, heighten the conflict among social groups, each struggling to improve its real living standard. Continued poor productivity performance would also eliminate our capacity to address any important issue on our national social agenda that requires the deployment of new resources.

It is, however, useful to note that the post-1973 productivity slowdown occurred, to some extent, almost everywhere in the industrial world. If we compare the annual rates of productivity growth in the two periods 1965–73 and 1973–79, we find that Japan "slowed" from 9.1 to 3.4 percent, Germany from 4.3 to 3.1 percent, the United Kingdom from 3.4 to 1.1 percent, and the United States from 1.6 to 0.3 percent. Moreover, what economists (or others) actually know about productivity growth over time, and across countries, does not adequately explain our empirical observations. We lack a thorough understanding of interfirm differences in productivity, and we comprehend even less about the complex processes that generate, evaluate, then spread the adaptation of new technologies. Yet it is this critical step—the successful adaptation of new technologies—that produces major social and economic dividends.

What is needed to bring about economic growth and job development? I would identify three important and proximate causes: (1) the educational attainment and health of the work force; (2) capital growth, that is, the growth of plant machinery and equipment; and (3) technological advances. These are not separate, independent factors but rather interact with one another. The more capital growth there is, the more technological advances there will be; the more technological advances are achieved, the greater the capital growth, and so on. Such interactions among educational attainment, capital growth, and technological advances generate economic growth. These factors have been studied in many countries over long periods of time and, although there is some argument over how important each one is relative to the others, it is clear that these three comprise the key elements involved in economic growth.

Two other factors affect growth more indirectly: first, the changing composition of industry, for example from agriculture to manufacturing; second, the nature of existing social, political, and economic institutions. Technological and scientific advancement can create opportunities for us but cannot, by themselves, create economic growth. How workers are used, how firms are organized, how employers and employees work together, and how our gross national product is distributed all help determine whether we gain the potential available from technological and scientific advances. The successful exploitation of new scientific understanding is critically dependent on the adaptability of our economic, social, and political institutions, our attitudes toward work and change, and many other cultural issues. In short, there is a long and tortuous path leading from discoveries in the laboratory to activities that actually affect productivity, welfare, and economic growth.

As in the recipe for a cake, all these ingredients, whether proximate or indirect, must work together. Educational attainment, investment and capital, and technological advances must be deployed in a dynamic industrial sector for which an appropriate set of social and political institutions has developed in order to achieve economic growth or job development.

Out of this complex of factors necessary to economic growth, technological advances merit further attention because it is the successful development and implementation of new technologies that will largely determine any country's economic success in the years ahead. Technological progress has been, I believe, one of the great liberating forces in Western civilization—certainly in contemporary Western civilization.

Technological change is not simply the exchange of one nuisance for another, as skeptics claim. It does not destroy jobs but creates them. Even more important is its potential for what I call the "enhanced exchange" of jobs, the possibility of exchanging spirit-breaking labor for work that can expand our human potential rather than draining it. Technological progress does, at times, carry with it unexpected and undesirable side effects, which certainly need to be confronted and may even prove intolerable. But these should not blind us to the great advantage of technological progress and economic development: they are what give us the basic ability to address our social agenda.

How are technological developments encouraged? This controversial issue has been studied in many dimensions: across countries, within countries, between industries, and so on. In the considerable literature on the topic, three conditions stand out as strongly associated with periods of rapid technological advances. One is adequate investment in research and development. Undeniably, science can only be generated through the practice of science, and this requires a substantial investment in research and development. Sadly, the resources that the federal government invests in research and development (as a percentage of gross national product) have dwindled in the last fifteen years. Second, and often overlooked, are the numerous technological advances that can be characterized as "learning-by-doing." While many technological advances come directly from the laboratory, many others come from practical activities in the plant as we design and install new equipment or solve production problems. The magnitude of this type of technological advance is directly related to the overall rate of economic activity. The better the economy is doing, the more new technology will be stimulated in this way. Third, as data from different industries and countries attest, technological development occurs in environments with strong bases in science and engineering.

Turning back from these general considerations to the particular circumstances of the U.S. economy in the last decade, we find that five kinds of explanation are usually offered for declines in productivity growth. The first is low levels of savings and/or investment. It is often argued that aspects of our tax system now encourage Americans to consume too much and to save and invest too little. Low rates of investment and the subsequent lowering of the amount of capital per worker lead to a decrease in productivity. These unfortunate biases in our tax laws, it is argued, became exaggerated in the inflationary environment of the 1970s.

A second explanation, the changing quality and composition of the labor force, has not been a critical issue in the 1973–79 period. Nor is there much evidence to support a third explanation, decline in technological innovation. Although it is difficult to assess this accurately, new technological development does not seem to have changed appreciably in this period.

A fourth causal factor offered to explain the fall in productivity growth is the energy crisis. The rapidly rising price of oil is thought to have hampered productivity growth in four different but interrelated ways: (1) new oil prices made a significant part of our capital stock unprofitable to use and thus lowered the effective capital/labor ratio; (2) a significant amount of effort was transferred from production to energy conservation; (3) the energy crisis slowed the overall force of economic activity and thus eliminated certain possibilities for productivity enhancement; (4) uncertainty about the continued flow of energy caused an inefficient reallocation of resources on a geographic basis (e.g., "premature" abandonment of factories in energy-poor areas). Indeed, the energy crisis may be the most important *single* cause of the productivity slowdown in the United States and other oil-importing industrial states.

A fifth cause cited for the productivity slowdown is the "burden" of government regulations (e.g., the Occupational Safety and Health Administration created in 1970; the Clean Air Act of 1970, the Noise Control Act of 1972, the Toxic Substances Act of 1976), which divert resources from the production of measured output toward the production of unmeasured output, such as safety or pollution control. The problem here may be in the way we measure productivity growth. If our gross national product accounts were credited with the benefits of these regulatory programs, we might find ourselves better off than we now believe we are. To the extent that these programs are either ill-designed or poorly run, however, they represent a deadweight loss to the economy.

Thus among the five explanations usually advanced for a decline in productivity growth, the last two—the energy crisis and government regulation—seem the most credible. The 1970s apparently witnessed an important structural change in the U.S. economy—one instigated by the energy crisis and perhaps abetted by the onset of increased government regulation of the economy. These events may have rendered a nontrivial part of our human and nonhuman capital stock obsolete. If so, much of the creative potential of U.S. industry was absorbed in adapting to difficult circumstances rather then breaking ahead into new territory. As for the future, we must rededicate our efforts to improving not only the scientific and engineering base of our economy but our understanding of the human/social/political factors that also make economic growth possible.

Michigan Can Manufacture
a Solid Future

Contemporary public policy discussions are full of rhetoric about the importance of science and technology to national and regional economic growth and about the need for a new "industrial policy" to meet the challenges of the next decades. This interest is justified even though the rhetoric is, at best, often superficial.

In the years ahead the pace of change in technology and science will accelerate, and the changes will be more revolutionary than ever before. As individuals and communities, we must develop new and socially acceptable methods of adapting to change. If successful change is to occur, it must be equitable as well as efficient.

In addition, most of the new developments in science and technology will be multinational in origin; that is, no nation will be able to generate or keep pace with tomorrow's complex technologies on its own. Scientists, engineers, workers, and managers must enter this new era of cooperation on both a domestic and an international basis. Our competitiveness in international markets and our efficiency in domestic areas will become more dependent on the use to which we put new technologies and the social, political, and economic changes that must accompany such developments.

What does this mean for Michigan? Manufacturing has traditionally been the most important industry in Michigan. If we wish to remain a relatively high-income region, manufacturing must remain the most important industry in Michigan. The economic challenge before this state is not to diversify our industry from high-wage sectors to low-wage sectors. Low wages are better than no wages, it is true, but they hardly constitute an objective worthy of either our inheritance (human, physical, and financial assets) or our potential. Rather, the challenge for the citizens of this state is to help support an environment of continuing innovation that can generate increases in productivity and, thus, sustain high real incomes.

Given our history, our resources, and our location, such gains are, in my opinion, most likely to be achieved and sustained by assuming worldwide leadership in the manufacturing sector. This is not to say that agriculture, tourism, and other industries— particularly financial and health services—are unimportant to Michigan, but they cannot be expected to provide a level of continuing change in productivity and production that will support above-average incomes over long periods of time.

The most recent recession in manufacturing has sent most national and regional observers scurrying in the wrong direction. At the national level, a premature funeral has been held for American manufacturing. Although it has been hard hit in the early 1980s by both recession and the very strong dollar, manufacturing continues to generate new jobs and new technology. If the national public policy debate would shift from vague discussions of industrial policy toward a consideration of the more traditional macroeconomic goals (i.e., growth, balance of payments, inflation, etc.), the "revitalization" of manufacturing—through economic growth and a more realistically valued dollar—would occur.

In Michigan much public rhetoric calls for the diversification of the state's industry. This is an understandable goal, reflecting a natural desire to shield the state's economy from the inevitable cyclical ups and downs of durable goods production. But diversification becomes much less attractive if we move beyond a superficial analysis and recognize the genuine underlying vitality of much of U.S. manufacturing.

There are high-wage jobs outside manufacturing, but Michigan is unlikely to become a national center of such activity. There are many low-wage jobs outside of manufacturing that might be relatively easy to attract. We should not, however, devote our "first-line" energy to such an effort. Instead, we—management, labor, government, and education—should face the challenge of making Michigan the center of creative innovation in manufacturing again.

Change will be required to accomplish this revitalization, and change has already begun. Some of the new requirements will be: (1) a highly trained work force—including managers—that will eagerly adapt to change and commit itself to a continuous process of learning and leadership; (2) a new and strengthened relationship between the state's research universities and business enterprises; (3) a commitment to international standards of excellence in the import, export, and production of new ideas and products; (4) public awareness that a social agenda requires real resources that can be provided only by overall economic productivity; (5) an understanding by the electorate that public goods are a critical aspect of a society's capacity to work together. Narrowness of purpose and protectionism of self-interest—at home or abroad—may well be self-defeating. In the final analysis, we citizens of Michigan must create our own wealth and not expect others to support us.

Technological change has always been an important component of economic growth, but in the next decades it will become increasingly central and even more closely related to current science. To operate successfully in this environment will require effective communication not only between scientists and engineers at home but also with the worldwide community of scientists, engineers, suppliers, and customers. In addition, it will require social and political commitments appropriate to this new environment. In Michigan's traditional area of expertise—manufacturing—we must strive for and attain leadership.

The Economic Program of the Reagan Administration

With the election of President Reagan we may have come to a significant turning point in our national life. Over the last few years Americans have suffered a growing unhappiness with national policy, particularly economic policy and the role of the federal government. A mounting sentiment calls for a new approach to the challenges of inflation, productivity, energy, poverty, health care, defense, and other matters on the "unfinished agenda" of national objectives. This national sentiment, at least in part, calls into question what is perceived to be our overly ambitious and expansionary policies of the last two decades. In the view of the Reagan Administration, these policies have simply interfered with the natural and efficient market mechanisms of the private sector and have caused our "stagflation."

President Reagan's program clearly represents a bold departure from the "Great Society" approach, advocating as it does a series of policies designed, at the very least, to transfer income, wealth, and power from the public to the private sector. As I understand it, the overall objective of his economic program is to restore a stable framework of private incentives and price signals that will then deal effectively with many social problems that have continued to defy previous efforts to grapple with them. These new initiatives come at a time when there is widespread disappointment in the performance of the U.S. economy and in the actual achievements of the Great Society, especially the role of certain federal transfer payment programs.

The Administration's new policies seem to be based, in part, on these premises: (1) market failures are less troublesome than failures of government policy; (2) government initiatives in many areas are bound to fail; (3) the larger the federal budget, the lower the growth potential of the economy; (4) the "trickling down" effect is better than broad social programs; and (5) the amount of creative effort that Americans put forth directly corresponds to their after-tax income, and may be inversely related to the adequacy of the "safety net" available to the economy's "dropouts."

One useful window on the Administration's economic policy is its proposed federal budget. In terms of budget policy, the program seems to rest on three major pillars: (1) considerably increased expenditures in the national defense area, (2) a sharp slowdown in the rate of growth of nondefense expenditures, and (3) substantial cuts in taxes, including a 30 percent cut in personal income tax rates over a three-year period. There are, of course, other important aspects of the Administration's economic program (e.g., new regulatory policy, incentives for savings and investments), but these three issues, together with a monetary policy characterized by modest growth in the money supply, will have the determining impact on the evolution of the U.S. economy in the early 1980s.

Behind all such economic premises and policies lies a vision. Beginning in the 1960s, the vision of the Great Society was grounded on the perception that poverty and unemployment were involuntary occupations. Its programs were largely strategies to remedy this situation. Whether or not all the strategies were successful, they certainly had some unexpected side effects, and many of the key current objectives of national economic policy are designed to cope with these.

Further, the Administration's economic program is based on its judgment of what the economic, social, and political priorities of the American people are. Economists often overlook the social and political "baggage" that inheres in all economic policies. But we must evaluate the Administration's policies in precisely these terms, not just in terms of balanced budgets, inflation, and employment. These policies reflect how we see ourselves as people and how we wish others to see us. Let me offer some examples.

One critical question in this respect is: What motivates work and creative effort in Americans? More specifically, to what extent are work effort, productivity, and savings motivated by after-tax income? "Reaganomics" or "supply-side economics" claims that, at current prices, wage rates, taxes, and other incentives, no further production can be coaxed out of the American economy. In essence, this implies—in contrast to the Great Society stance—that poverty and unemployment (of both labor and capital) are voluntary occupations.

With respect to implementation strategies, we should ask ourselves exactly which current activities of the federal government we wish to curtail. We all wish to eliminate waste, but after that, how do we feel about trade-offs among such expenditures as: support of the elderly through Social Security; support of the sick through Medicaid; support of infants and young people through food stamps, school lunches, and education; support of scientific research through the National Institutes of Health, the National Science Foundation, etc.; farm supports; support of anticompetitive practices in construction, maritime affairs, and health care delivery. Many other, perhaps more important, issues could be raised. My point is not so much to answer these particular questions as to encourage debate within a framework that emphasizes significant value judgments.

There are, I believe, a number of problems with the Administration's economic program. Perhaps the greatest of these is that any damage it might do will not be clear until the federal budget is thoroughly dismantled. At that point we might find ourselves with lower taxes but an unacceptable impotency to act on critical social problems.

There are other problems as well. Although a political consensus seems to favor tax cuts, there is no current political agreement on any given area to target for substantial budget reductions. We all want energy independence, for example, but no one is willing to sacrifice anything for it. This asymmetry could lead to much *larger* government deficits unless we take steps to avoid such an undesirable outcome. If we believe a smaller government would serve our best interests in the long run and help release the creative efforts of the American people, we must be prepared to designate which current government activities to phase out. Since 90 to 92 percent of the federal budget is already earmarked for defense, entitlement programs, or interest on the government debt, these decisions will be especially difficult and are likely to be unpopular. The size of the budget deficit bequeathed by the Carter Administration—perhaps $100 billion—only complicates the predicament.

Another problem is that tax cuts seem extremely unlikely to stimulate the massive "incentive" response that would be required in order to generate needed tax revenues and move the budget toward balance. Cuts in personal taxes would, I expect, have a modest impact on the quantity and quality of work effort supplied to the market at existing wages, but that impact would be much too small even to begin to balance the federal budget in the next few years.

We might ask, in this context, whether the Reagan economic program is credible as an anti-inflation program. Although a budget deficit of $100 billion may seem inflationary to some, this need not be the outcome. Large tax cuts will put considerable resources in private hands, and the government will have the opportunity to finance the deficit by issuing debt rather than by monetary expansion. Furthermore, foreign savings may be mobilized to finance our deficit. Even if the deficit is financed by the issuance of debt (domestic or foreign), however, there might be a secondary effect on productivity as the federal government crowds out the private sector from capital markets.

Thus current Administration policies will yield rapidly rising federal deficits, potentially high interest rates, and a weaker than necessary economic recovery. Moreover, in an age of ever-stronger political and economic links with our trading partners, all of these domestic tendencies could be exaggerated by recessions abroad, sharp inflows of foreign capital, and an even stronger U.S. dollar. Our increasing economic interdependence will work to spread and prolong any economic recession or slowdown unless we develop more cooperative international policies than we now have. Indeed, I would predict that the "spreading" effects of an economic slowdown might well cause an international monetary crisis by impairing the ability of debtor countries to meet their obligations.

In the defense area, assuming for the moment the advisability of strengthening our international position and our national defense posture, I would question whether the Administration's program is the most effective means of achieving this objective. There are, I suggest, four preconditions to a viable national defense, and I will address them in order of priority. The first is a domestic political consensus on the aims of our defense efforts. Any precipitous attempt to dismantle the existing relative priorities in the federal budget will, I believe, erode the political support for other elements (e.g., defense) of the Administration's program. It is a matter not of the size of the federal budget but of the relative balance among the various categories. This balance has been forged on the anvil of national debate over decades. It may be time to change direction, but there are potential political dangers in changing too quickly.

The support of our allies is a second precondition to a successful national defense policy. Given existing international monetary arrangements, a chronic inflation in the U.S. transmits delicate political decisions to our allies. It also creates difficulties for our friends in OPEC. If we use up our measure of goodwill in such accommodations, we have less to expend in attracting allies to objectives in the defense area. Thus we might greatly increase allied support for our international position by restoring price stability at home. Unfortunately, our current defense proposals may make it more difficult to control domestic inflation and so may jeopardize our capacity to gain the support of our allies.

The third priority for an effective defense is a strong economy. To the extent, therefore, that the Reagan program fails to restore price stability and economic growth, it undermines the base of any strong defense posture. The fourth and last priority is an effective, well-equipped armed force, and this seems to be the only prerequisite that the Reagan program addresses.

Until the first three priorities for a strong defense can be achieved, a massive infusion of new government spending in this area may be premature. There are other reasons to favor a slower rise in defense expenditures as well. It is not clear that we know how to effectively spend such large increases in a short period of time. In addition there are presently many bottlenecks in the defense supply industry and limits on how quickly certain components of our armed forces can be reoriented. Most importantly, in an era of rapidly escalating nuclear peril we still have too many unanswered strategic questions.

Besides a slower rise in defense expenditures, I would recommend two modifications in President Reagan's tax reduction program. My proposal is designed to achieve the Administration's stated goals—namely, to cure inflation, strengthen our international position, and decrease the size of government—but it involves a phased accomplishment of these objectives. Any attempt to achieve them in "one brilliant stroke" is too risky and will, in my opinion, fail. My first recommendation is to consider immediate tax reductions only in the areas that offer direct incentives for saving and investment. If personal tax rates must be cut, we should increase other taxes, perhaps adopting a value-added tax. My second recommendation is to consider broad-based cuts in personal income tax only after stability is restored in capital markets and inflation seems credibly to have receded. For the short run, I prefer a somewhat tighter fiscal policy, and a somewhat looser monetary policy—one that is better coordinated with that of West Germany, Japan, and Great Britain. This program of a more moderate buildup in the defense budget and phased tax cuts is not as stimulating in the short run as President Reagan's, but I believe it is more likely to restore stability and growth to the system in the mid-term.

Finally, whatever the appropriate structure of current economic policy, we should remember that economic policies do not work quickly. They begin to take effect only when economic units come to believe that a new policy is *permanently* in place. The problems afflicting the U.S. economy in the early 1980s have been building for two decades, and they will not be quickly cured.

Implications of
Changing Technologies

Public Policy and the International Transfer of Technology

The last decades have witnessed the widespread adoption of "high technology" through technology transfer, international finance, and vastly improved communications and transportation. There has also been a significant and continuous geographical shift of production capacities and activities. These developments have ignited widespread concern for the stability of existing income shares and a new interest in protectionism with respect to the international flow of goods and services, capital, and technology. In the United States this rising tide of protectionism reflects a growing concern that our traditional free trade strategy may be inappropriate to currently evolving world production patterns and to trading partners that behave "unfairly."

Protectionism is not a new theme, although the current focus on the international flow of technology—the newest instrument of national policy—gives contemporary discussions a distinctive character. Historically, strong political forces have always mobilized to protect either the short-term or long-term special interest (i.e., "monopoly" rents) of particular groups. As W. M. Corden has pointed out, national governments usually do not allow shifting patterns of international trade to rapidly alter the real income of any significant group in the economy. In addition, governments have employed both tariff and nontariff barriers to exploit a perceived national monopoly in technology, raw materials, or other production factors and to build or protect a national capacity in a particular area. In such cases it is usually argued either that the resultant "monopoly" prices exact a "tax" from foreign customers that more than compensates for the higher price, poorer quality, and smaller variety available to domestic consumers in the protected market itself or that some dimension of the national welfare, such as national security, demands a sacrifice. Ironically, when increasingly popular nontariff barriers are used, foreign suppliers may capture some of the resultant "monopoly" rents or windfall gains, as with the current auto quotas in the United States. This may help explain the cooperation of foreign producers, and it does avoid General Agreement on Tariffs and Trade negotiations. But the cost is an even greater distortion of world trading patterns.

Economists have been virtually unanimous in their support for free trade, or at least for a set of policies promoting the efficient allocation of world resources. They have, however, based many of their most powerful insights and policy prescriptions on a static world of perfectly competitive markets. Perhaps partly for this reason, their advice has been steadfastly ignored despite their more recent insights into optimal public policy for a world of imperfectly competitive markets and less than "statesmanlike" trading partners.

These newer directions in economic theory are important because they bear on the current industrial structure, which is dominated by forces quite different from those that produce a world of perfect competition. These forces include: economies of scale and scope (including managerial skills), uncertainty, entry barriers (including access to technology), learning by doing, product differentiation, marketing and other consortia, and tariff barriers. In such environments even economists will acknowledge that free trade may not be appropriate public policy for a particular country. In the presence of scale economies, for example, public policies aimed at the protection of domestic markets and promotion of exports may reduce per unit costs and save resources. In such cases, monopoly rents can potentially be kept at home, especially if market entry requires large investments. When possible retaliation by foreign governments is factored in, however, the nature of the net gain becomes unclear.

The historical record is clear in at least one respect: economic efficiency is not the only goal of public policy. Most governments exhibit only limited commitment to the international division of labor and its resulting economic efficiencies and long-run real income benefits. Governments often seem to prefer the more expensive policy of self-sufficiency and the short-term protection of existing domestic income shares. As a result, economists have recently become more interested in the political economy of protectionism. Further, they increasingly recognize that in a world of large trading partners with varying policies toward international trade, it may be necessary to develop national policies that are not directly consistent with a liberal international trading environment.

In response to these realities economists are, through the theory of the second best, beginning to consider optimal public policy in the presence of broad classes of market distortions. Many would argue, for example, that it may be necessary to impose various retaliatory protectionist measures as part of the dynamic by which we move from the current unstable environment to a more mutually beneficial cooperative arrangement.

Because of possible production or consumption externalities, adjustment costs, and broad strategic concerns between trading partners, there are, I believe, appropriate occasions for a policy of at least transitory protection. Nonetheless, I remain skeptical of the long-run benefits of protectionist policies, especially as they affect the free flow of information and technology across international boundaries. In the context of the market structures and institutional arrangements that will probably dominate the next decades, traditional economic theory can provide only limited assistance in the formation of overall public policy. More recent initiatives are encouraging but not yet adequately developed.

Rather than focusing on either the conventional or the newer economic arguments, this essay will suggest that the expected nature of technological developments and the potential pace of their implementation over the next decades substantially increase the incentive to international cooperation in the formation of public policy. By international cooperation, I mean the mutual avoidance among trading partners of policies that distort the world allocation of resources. In particular, I will argue that constellations of national public policies that inhibit the international flow of technology are self-defeating and that pursuit of narrowly defined short-term self-interest by each country will leave all worse off.

This argument applies especially to the advanced countries among whom the technological gaps have considerably narrowed, but it is, I believe, also valid for advancing countries, given the technologies they will wish to implement. To serve the long-term self-interest of all countries, public policy should follow the path pointed by the private sector, which, with somewhat narrower objectives, is already beginning to behave cooperatively. The difficulty is that prices set by private firms may or may not adequately meet the costs of the technology transfer or international joint ventures they undertake. Goods, wealth, and technology—whether public or private—need not be transferred at zero prices, but I believe it is too costly for public policy to inhibit such movements systematically. In the coming years, public policy will be challenged to address the longer term issues and anticipate the special nature of future technological and organizational reality.

In a world composed of trading partners with vastly different institutional arrangements, the objective of establishing mutually beneficial public policies will be challenging indeed. Such an objective is difficult enough to achieve in areas like monetary policy, but the areas of science and technology present additional quandaries. If, for example, all countries treated research and development (including advanced training) as public investments and their outputs, therefore, as public goods, the challenge of ensuring equitable cost-sharing for research and development would still be substantial. But such investments are public in some countries and private in others, presenting a challenge that quite surpasses the operation and pricing of private markets. If one country treats advanced research training and basic scientific research as a public good and a trading partner treats them as private investments, private markets alone may not generate appropriate transfer prices. Public policies must confront such issues since major trade flows occur among countries with widely different socioeconomic arrangements and varying commitments to private markets.

These issues relating to international trade and technology transfer are fundamentally linked to national concerns of economic growth and technological change. We turn now to the nexus of all these issues.

Technology, Economic Growth, and the International Transfer of Technology: Then and Now

There is currently great interest in the varying ability among nations to mobilize their innovative capacities effectively. Cumulative changes in technology and social organization have clearly transformed the human condition, but our preoccupation with technology-related issues is unusual, recalling a similar concern during the early stage of the Industrial Revolution.

Different societies have always had varying abilities to generate or adopt economically and socially useful innovations and to conceive or implement new ideas. The slow and uneven diffusion of new knowledge throughout history simply cannot be explained by the economic categories of cost and uncertainty alone. Now that instantaneous worldwide communication has created a common knowledge base, the extremely diverse capacities of various nations to implement even well-understood production techniques appears even more puzzling.

The current concern is not narrowly focused on a nation's capacity in basic science but on the ability to identify, to develop, and, most importantly, to implement new techniques that have meaningful economic or social payoffs. It is only implementation that actually generates economic growth. Every national government now seems intent on ensuring a national capacity for continuing technological innovation. Most understand, as Joseph A. Schumpeter noted decades ago, that meaningful payoffs accrue only to economies with an ongoing ability to innovate, since the social and/or economic payoffs of any single innovation are usually small. Real changes in productivity result from a complex, reinforcing system that supports many new innovations, large and small, organizational and technical.

Governments, rulers, and other administrative hierarchies have always understood at least some of the potential advantages of technological change. But only recently have these changes assumed such a strategically central role that political leaders throughout the world are examining not only the economic and social impact of technological innovation but the process by which such changes occur. Advanced and developing countries alike now consider the capacity to identify, develop, and implement socially and economically useful new technologies as strategically crucial to ensuring stable economic growth and, in some cases, national security.

This attitude reflects a new awareness that rapidly changing, highly sophisticated technologies—relying increasingly on science—will underlie virtually all new economic activity of any scale. In short, competitiveness in international markets and cost-effectiveness in domestic ones both depend increasingly on the continuous implementation of new technologies.

It is interesting to speculate on why so much is expected of new technology in the next decades. It is true that unprecedented advances in science have marked the last twenty years, but the moderate rate of growth in productivity has not been exceptional. Although our productivity measures may be downwardly biased because meaningful changes in quality are difficult to incorporate, many observers would warn against expecting more from science in the coming years. I disagree. The critical new dimension of the next decades will be the new synergetic and more productive relationship among science, technological innovation, and the implementation of new technology.

This expected new era in the relationship of science, technology, and economic growth coincides with yet another new characteristic of national economies throughout the industrialized world: the increasing internationalization of world markets. A growing proportion of world production is moving across international boundaries and making national markets increasingly interdependent. Furthermore, capital and technology are moving between markets at an unprecedented rate and with an unparalleled freedom. Multinational corporations are, of course, playing a critical role in much of this movement. Technology itself is being moved across international boundaries through many vehicles, including trade flows (technology embodied in product), licensing agreements, foreign direct investment, consulting, migration of skilled labor, training of foreign students, scientific exchanges, and the openness of scientific and technological literature. Predicting increasingly important and rapidly evolving technologies and anticipating greater interdependence in world markets, national governments are reassessing public policy toward technology, international trade, and international technology transfer.

Despite these new conditions, the current debate suffers from being ahistorical. Although distinguished by their focus on technology and technology transfer, the general public policy issues involved are traditional. In this new environment, we are again asking the old question: Is our national welfare advanced by an open, mutually beneficial policy of trade and technology transfer, or can we serve our own national interests best by a public policy that, for example, attempts to create a monopoly in technology that can be exploited to our long-run benefit? This assessment of overall national welfare is, of course, always complicated by regard for the interests of particular political coalitions.

Public attention to the links among technical progress, economic growth, trade, and the international transfer of technology goes back to ancient times. Indeed, the early river valley civilizations of the Middle East concerned themselves with these very issues. They enjoyed some of the economic, political, and military benefits of technological change and new organizational structures. Moreover, regional shortages of raw materials, food, forage, and "know-how" produced a thriving structure of interregional trade in goods, services, and technology. The most common vehicle for interregional technology transfer at that time was the movement of skilled labor.

Even in these early days of Middle Eastern history, the development of new technologies, the diffusion of technology, and trade flows all exerted a major influence on the economic, social, and political evolution of the societies in this region. The development of the hub wheel, the chariot, and the compound bow, for example, affected patterns of world trade, political dominance, and the international distribution of wealth and power. Although armed raids often substituted for trade in goods and technology, trade nevertheless became the predominant foundation for economic growth and international relations. As soon as societies advanced out of subsistence economies, technology, trade, and technology transfer became issues of public policy. Indeed the history of technical progress, international technology transfer, and trade cannot be separated from the history of civilization itself, since it explores two issues critical to every society: (1) the effort to master the environment by managing the forces of nature in a manner that augments productivity (technical progress) and (2) the sharing of economic capacity and the spread of new knowledge (trade and technology transfer). Thus, these subjects are as old as civilization. But our interest in them has revived because we anticipate a more rapidly developing technology, an increasingly complex dialectic between technology and science, and a decreasing lag between new developments in technology and their implications for national security.

Some Selected Myths

In revisiting these ancient issues, however, we encounter a number of myths clouding the various relationships among science, technology creation, technology utilization, international technology transfer, economic growth, and national security. These must be dispelled before a more direct analysis of the issues can be undertaken. The four myths I will address are the scientific myth, the technology king myth, the technology closet myth, and the technology defense myth.

The *scientific myth* refers to the idea that new science always precedes new technological innovations, marching to the beat of its own "drummer." This myth holds that basic research makes new discoveries about the underlying forces of nature and thus enables new technological developments.

In fact, however, the complex association between science and technology is not unidirectional. History amply demonstrates that an operating but poorly understood technology can have important economic consequences and can directly affect the subsequent scientific agenda. The development of the software industry—without any science—is a contemporary example. Far from being independent, the scientific agenda reflects the influence of technology and is therefore directly related to economic forces like relative prices and aggregate demand. In addition, numerous scientific experiments have had to await further developments in technology. Many economic historians have observed that innovation often responds to the "pull" of the market. We must also see that basic science responds, in part, to the same set of economic forces. Strong economic growth, for example, greatly stimulates progress in both technological innovation and basic science.

If civilization had waited for a full comprehension of the underlying science before implementing a technology, we would have experienced only a small fraction of the economic growth we have actually achieved. Nathan Rosenberg, among others, has reminded us that the science of thermodynamics grew out of an attempt to understand the efficiency of the steam engine, that many of

Pasteur's important discoveries emerged from an effort to solve production problems in the wine industry, and that we had extensive experience with semiconductors before we grasped the source of their special properties. Other examples range from the sailboat to the telephone. Moreover, leadership in basic science is clearly insufficient for leadership in the implementation of new ideas. In fact, the pace of technological innovation is often dictated by events in one country and the pace of developments in basic science by events in another. Scientific leadership may produce a competitive edge and thus be a good investment, but it is not enough to ensure success.

The next myth, the *technology king myth*, holds that a new technological idea can, by itself, release a new level of productivity and economic growth. Yet in fact, a vast gulf separates the development of a new idea from its actual implementation, which depends on a wide spectrum of technological challenges, the perceived economic or social payoff, and important nontechnological characteristics such as human behavior, motivation, and overall social organization. Historically, the ability to implement socially and economically useful new ideas has always been related to overarching societal factors, not simply to technical expertise.

This point is well illustrated by three innovations fundamental to much of post-Renaissance technological development in Western Europe: printing, gunpowder, and the compass. All three were invented in China but only exploited in a meaningful economic way in Western Europe. Similarly, Daniel Boorstin's comparison in *The Discoverers* of the European to the Chinese development of the clock highlights the great impact of societal attitudes on the diffusion of a new technology. In China the technology of the clock, used to help construct the special dynastic calendars, was a secret closely guarded by the emperor's personal staff. In Europe the clock was first used to call the public to worship; it quickly became a public good, to the enormous benefit of much subsequent Western technology.

Two lessons emerge from these examples. First, a country's technological dynamism depends on many of its nontechnological characteristics. It is, for example, crucial that Western religions taught us to escape current experience by trying to comprehend its underlying meaning rather than by waiting for a better cycle of events to occur. This outlook helped us move from experience to experiments. Second, a country's technological dynamism can grow or decline during different periods as a function of a broad set of social and economic traits.

According to the *technology closet myth*, substantial benefits accrue to the country that develops a new idea if public policy can ensure regional control of the relevant information. In a simple, homogeneous world there would be no reason for public policy to restrict the movement of knowledge as long as we allowed for "lump sum" incentive payments to the developers of new technology. Nor would such restrictions be necessary if all firms were multinationals and were owned in completely multinational fashion, or if there were truly integrated international equity markets. In real life, however, we inhabit a world in which our trading partners are often both customers and competitors, to say nothing of their potential military relations with us. In such a world we must at least ask whether our national interest calls for a protective policy that would exploit the profits from our technology, or other special skills, and, if so, how to achieve it. Our national interest could of course include income distribution objectives, both at home and abroad.

Two processes work against the technology closet myth. First, most technological barriers have proven quite porous. Despite many attempts to block it, technology has managed to cross all barriers erected by public policy long before full monopoly rents could be earned. The central challenge for "foreign competitors" has not been access to new knowledge but organizational or factor supply impediments to the implementation of new ideas. The great Portuguese navigators hid their navigational charts and still lost the oceans. Admiral Drake hid his and no one could find them.

Second, most meaningful technological innovations involve a continuous process of change—a process jeopardized by too much secrecy. Secrecy does build monopolies, but monopolies build further secrecy and finally inefficiency. Innovation proceeds most efficiently when new products and ideas are subject to the widest possible exposure, to criticism not only from scientists and engineers but from supplier and customer markets worldwide. Effective technology cannot long be closeted, and the cost is usually not worth the benefit anyway. In the end we must count on a continuous capacity for successful innovation.

The *national security myth* claims that new and advanced technology is the key to maintaining an edge in national security.

Here again, history indicates that more advanced technology, while it can be critical, must be accompanied by a social support system that renders it credible and effective. Early Moslem victories, for instance, depended more on social discipline and shared objectives than on superior technology. The same was true of the Assyrian armies and the Mongol "hordes" of the Great Khan. Modern technology may have replaced personal prowess and honor on the battlefield, but it has not replaced the extensive logistical and administrative requirements and the social cohesion necessary to effective military management.

As is apparent from my choice of myths, I would argue against the easy adoption of protectionist measures in high technology industries, particularly those measures that might hinder the flow of information across international boundaries. Let me return briefly to the insights of economic theory to illuminate this argument.

Economic Issues

Economists have produced a large literature on technological change, but most of it concerns the effect of newly implemented technologies on output, employment, prices, and the distribution of income and wealth. Only a small portion examines the process of technological innovation and how this process relates to international flows of goods, services, capital, labor, or technology. Even this portion does not very helpfully address the relationship of developing technologies to the changing structure of markets, let alone other social organizations.

The pure theory of international trade supplies a little additional insight. According to this theory, a new innovation changes factor and product prices and may or may not positively affect the innovating center, assuming the comparatively static general equilibrium world of perfect competition. In this environment the innovation itself cannot influence the market power of the firm. For most observers and businesspeople, however, it is precisely this change in market power that motivates the whole process of innovation. The challenge, as perceived by market participants, is to decide when to make a permanent set of resource commitments for the purpose of changing market power and capturing the resultant monopoly rents. Many of these issues are now being explored in the growing economic literature on the relationship between trade theory and industrial organization. These latest developments in economic theory are not complete, but initial insights seem to support the antiprotectionist bias of previous models, to point to optimal policy instruments, or to devise broad strategies for use in highly oligopolistic markets.

Today a significant proportion of international trade takes place in imperfectly competitive markets, even when technology is not critical (e.g., steel or automobiles), and such an environment produces a different pattern of prices, trade, and wealth than that engendered by the pure theory of international trade. So a different set of public policies may be appropriate.

International markets are not only imperfect; increasingly they are what some economists call "strategic oligopolies," meaning that a few large, interdependent economic units (firms, consortia of firms, or even governments) dominate trade flows. Appropriate public policies may be quite different in such environments, especially if governments are also acting as owner/managers of particular enterprises.

In a market with small numbers of large units, public policy can play an important role, but its impact will depend on the behavior (including induced responses) of foreign firms and foreign governments—which is not the case in perfectly competitive markets. The invisible hand (i.e., individual pursuit of self-interest) will work in this framework, but not perfectly, and only if private markets give adequate weight to the future. In the expected environment of most international trade flows, contemporary economic theory provides only a few clues. As a result, the welfare and efficiency consequences of international technology transfer are still being debated in established economic theory. The special nature of advanced technologies, however, suggests the appropriate bias for public policies.

The Special Nature of Advanced Technology

In the past, technical advances were transferred relatively simply, often through a few skilled laborers, a drawing, or a formula. Whatever the case, the transfer was generally a unitary process. Today, however, even a single product rests on sophisticated advances in a host of technologies. A jet engine, for instance, draws on combustion engineering, materials sciences, plasma physics, advanced forming and processing techniques, sensing and control devices, aerodynamics, and the systems know-how to mate engine to airframe. Not merely one or two of these technologies but all of them are vital to the successful implementation of jet engine technology.

To take another example, advances in the computer industry require expertise in design technologies, exotic materials, solid state physics, sophisticated processing and production techniques, information theory, specialized end-user knowledge, software design, programming and compilation, hardware-software interface know-how, and distribution and marketing skills. No nation is self-sufficient in information processing technologies.

Most new technologies have international rather than national origins and will depend on the international transfer of technology for their full development. Moreover, many technologies are devised for one purpose and then used mainly for another, making it difficult to predict which sector of the economy will fully exploit a particular technology. Public policy must, in my view, take into account this multiform, dynamic, and cross-fertilizing nature of advanced technology, recognizing that it can only be effectively transferred through deep, broad, and protracted relationships. The "Japanese" strategy of the last decades will no longer be feasible for advanced countries.

Information processing is the essence of scientific and technological change, given the anticipated pace of development. Effective, ongoing communication with other scientists and engineers, as well as with suppliers and customers, is a critical component of any organization that wishes to sustain its capacity for continuing innovation. Often the greatest obstacle to further discovery is the illusion of already possessing the needed knowledge. The protectionist approach, almost by definition, precludes that very flow which is so essential to technological progress and economic growth for all countries. If restrictive reciprocity should become the trend, all nations would suffer, but especially those whose technological development is not yet at least partially self-sustaining.

In sum, I believe that nations can no longer hope to generate or keep pace with today's technologies on their own. Even advanced countries can no longer alone match the international dynamics of technological progress; the technological gap among them is becoming too narrow and the technology too diverse. Those who envision the national development of advanced technologies behind protectionist walls may be deluding themselves.

Consequences and Choices

The new advanced technologies, which now underlie virtually all large-scale economic activity, will, I believe, originate in many countries and depend on multiple sources for their development. Their origins, development, and transfer will require a large measure of openness and encouragement, as well as institutional arrangements and public policies that ensure an equitable sharing of development costs. Now that national governments act as major market participants—investing in research and development (including training) and developing new technologies—public policy has acquired many new features.

Even in this new environment, 1 believe that restrictionism will retard the flow and development of new and advanced technology, affecting not only special technologies but the entire spectrum of economic effort and national security. Our mutual self-interest requires us to adapt to the inherent character of advanced technologies. We must encourage cross-fertilization, cross-border exchange, and flexibility. Our public policy toward science, technological development, and the international transfer of technology should reflect this new reality but should also, I believe, remain comparatively liberal and competitive, allowing market forces to guide firms in nationally and globally beneficial directions.

These comments leave open the critical question of just when public policies should intervene to steer the process of change, as well as the issues of which policy instruments can achieve the desired result and within what broad strategic framework. I hope the present discussion can help us approach these issues with a better understanding of the new and developing conditions of production.

The National Research Effort:
Funding and Policy Issues

The health of the scientific enterprise in the United States has become an important national concern. Indeed our international credibility and the vitality of our economy depend increasingly on developments in science and technology. The critical issue is whether the nation's scientific institutions and their patrons can mobilize and direct their efforts to support our national agenda. To do so, they must attend to such questions as: What new capital facilities (buildings and equipment) will be necessary to keep our research institutions competitive with those of other advanced countries? What national funding priorities should we set in order to ensure the optimal institutional arrangements for contemporary research? This paper considers aspects of both questions.

Let us turn first to the problem of capital facilities. While U.S. science and technology remain preeminent, our nation's capacity to produce new scientists and our university-based research facilities and equipment have been slowly eroding. At the same time our trading partners have rapidly increased their support for research and development, thus enhancing the vitality of their research institutions.

Since colleges and universities conduct a major share of basic research in the United States and virtually all the training of engineers and scientists, the quality of higher education's teaching and research laboratories is directly related to the training of our next generation of scientists and engineers and to the continued vitality of our nation's basic research effort.

Unfortunately, equipment in university laboratories—especially teaching laboratories—is much older than analogous equipment in most industrial and government settings. In the current environment of rapid technological change, this often renders university teaching laboratories obsolete. In fact, on a recent visit, scientists from China—not accustomed to using the latest scientific equipment—remarked that the laboratory of a leading university was the first place where they felt at home.

The teaching of science and engineering has always required equipment, but a number of new developments have strikingly accelerated the demand for up-to-date equipment in the classroom. First, the need to understand and use complex scientific instrumentation has expanded from the realm of basic research to the worlds of applied research, to industrial processes of all kinds and, more recently, to the implementation of such public policies as the assessment of toxic wastes. The ability to understand and use complex and rapidly changing equipment has become as critical to the engineer on the factory floor as to the scientist in the most advanced research laboratory. Employers of all kinds expect prospective personnel to be experienced in techniques requiring modern instrumentation. Students can only gain this knowledge in appropriately equipped teaching and research laboratories.

In chemistry, for example, the role of instrumentation has taken on an entirely new meaning. The revolution in analytical instrumentation has set qualitatively different equipment requirements and quantitatively different standards, not only for advanced research training and development and for the maintenance of modern industrial processes but also for meaningful undergraduate training. After decades of neglect and inadequate funding for educational institutions, the amount of new equipment needed for undergraduate instruction alone is staggering. To equip the nation's teaching laboratories properly would require a capital investment in the neighborhood of $3 billion and additional expenditures thereafter of $500 million a year.

A second development related to equipment needs is the increasingly central role of computers in our personal and professional lives and, therefore, in undergraduate instruction. To meet their educational obligations, universities and colleges must massively expand their investments in computer and communications equipment. Here also the challenge of keeping up to date is complicated by the extremely rapid changes in computer and communications technology and design and their frequent incompatibilities. A personal computer for each student is only the beginning. To make full use of the technology and develop students' awareness of its potential, networking or communication among computers is essential. Thus personal computers, microcomputers, minicomputers, and the mainframe installation must be interconnected to provide sufficient memory and speed of computation. In addition, software appropriate to meet teaching needs must be provided.

In some cases, computer technology can effectively compensate for the existing deficit in traditional laboratory equipment. The University of Michigan chemistry department, for example, has devised computer programs that teach students how to use pipettes, to titrate and perform other laboratory procedures, and to simulate certain experiments as well as the trial and error process of discovery. At the same time, the glaring deficiencies in laboratory equipment and scientific instrumentation may encourage too much dependence on computer simulation and analysis in undergraduate training at the expense of critical experiences in experimentation.

An improved capacity to train our physical and biological scientists will not alone serve to maintain our national leadership in science and technology. The successful application of scientific and technological advances, upon which our future economic vigor depends, also requires the research and insights of social scientists and humanists. For example, the extraordinary safety record of the U.S. aircraft industry can be ascribed to the joint contributions of physical and social scientists to the design of instrument and control systems. Such joint efforts will be more and more necessary as we move to newer technologies, such as advanced robotics.

It is, then, crucial for us to expose not only our aspiring scientists and engineers but also our social science and humanities students to the most recent trends in their disciplines. Historically, educators could count on only modest needs for equipment in fields outside of the natural sciences. But today the social sciences rely heavily upon statistical techniques, and the manipulation of large data bases has imposed a growing need for student access to computers in fields such as economics, sociology, business administration, library science, and psychology. In addition, the computer has become an invaluable accessory in such areas as language-teaching laboratories, linguistics, and text analysis in fields as disparate as English literature and biblical history.

One other capital resource necessary to our scientific progress and national well-being is also in danger of serious erosion: our university library collections. Book disintegration is a costly and pervasive problem that threatens the integrity of our historical records. Equally important, the information explosion of the last decades has far outrun the budgets of even our largest research libraries, so that recent acquisitions have been necessarily selective rather than comprehensive. Moreover, large expenditures are necessary to provide libraries with the requisite computing facilities and networking capacities to bring them into the information age. Without a timely infusion of funds, our libraries will no longer be adequate to our research and training needs.

Improving our campus research facilities will require new levels of support from government and private corporations that have a vested interest in the quality of university and college training. But equipment and materials comprise only one, albeit critical, component of a viable national effort in science and technology. We must also consider whether the new developments in these areas necessitate particular changes in the culture and structure of the research environment.

Under the leadership of Erich Bloch, the National Science Foundation (NSF) has been advocating a number of valuable new initiatives that address these structural issues but also require us to reconsider our national priorities in research funding. One such proposal is to devote more federal support to interdisciplinary and/or multidisciplinary research centers as against the more traditional individual investigator grant. I believe this initiative deserves careful evaluation.

Large, center-type grants to research institutions seem an appropriate strategy to pursue at this time. The call for interdisciplinary and/or multidisciplinary research is as old as the formation of scientific disciplines themselves. Specialization has had overwhelming benefits, but it has also defined a need to transcend its own boundaries. Indeed, the challenges of cooperative work among the specializations of a single discipline are as great as the challenge of cooperating across disciplines. The current NSF initiative, supported by similar efforts underway in many educational and research institutions, continues a long history of efforts to cross the traditional perimeters of knowledge.

Furthermore, many contemporary scientific discoveries are

available only through an interdisciplinary approach that would be difficult for an individual investigator to manage. In many fields we now require the merging of ideas, results, and techniques from separate disciplinary areas in order fully to exploit our scientific potential. In these areas the NSF initiative can be supportive and helpful.

Yet any revision of the culture and structure of what has been a very successful research environment ought to proceed cautiously and should not jeopardize the competitive individual investigator system which has served us so well. Thus, any expanded funding for research centers should be constrained by at least four considerations.

First, support for individual centers should be steady and predictable but time limited. Organizations, unlike individuals, create a bureaucratic capacity to sustain their support beyond their useful lifetime. It would be extremely unfortunate if NSF traded its future flexibility for a permanent commitment to a fixed group of centers.

Second, in many fields the interdisciplinary research center would not be the most effective way to organize research efforts. Selecting those scientific areas that could most profit from this form of support will require careful deliberation. Additionally, in areas where such research centers would be effective, the optimal forms (e.g., extent of industry participation) will vary widely. We should therefore encourage experimentation with different multidisciplinary models.

Third, we need to ensure that these research centers play their appropriate role in the education of the next generation of scientists and researchers. More attention must be paid to the potential synergy of such centers with both undergraduate and graduate education. We often speak of leveraging public research funds by also attracting private funds, but we frequently overlook the most important leverage facilitated by the public support of research: science education.

More broadly speaking, research centers that do not support the mission and values of the institution within which they operate will not prosper. It is thus crucial to structure these centers so that they reinforce rather than undermine faculty loyalties to the university as a coherent, interrelated academic community. They must, for instance, build on the merit and reward system already operating in the scholarly community rather than trying to proceed independently. Paradoxically, independence is riskier for a center than for an individual investigator.

Fourth, any research center must be firmly committed to the values of open communication and candid criticism, the cornerstone for the success of American science. Too much autonomy, security, secrecy, or insulation from open evaluation and criticism would greatly undermine a center's effectiveness.

One final *caveat* on the subject of funding research centers. The traditional strength of U.S. science and engineering research has been the individual investigator, and there is every reason to believe that the individual investigator will continue to be the principal source of new ideas. Thus the individual grant program needs to be protected and nourished, at least for the foreseeable future. Although the world of science and the nature of its supporting infrastructure have changed dramatically, the individual investigator program remains the environment most likely to foster the complex amalgam of competition, intellectual humility, open-mindedness, and risk taking so necessary to basic research.

The overriding goal of science policy is to assure that American science and the technology that both develops from it and supports it sustain our broad public purposes. These include national security, health, economic growth and competitiveness, the fuller realization of our individual potential, and the maintenance of our cultural and civic life. Science policy in America, especially since World War II, has been remarkably effective in helping our nation pursue these goals. If its success is to continue, we must carefully consider both how to renovate our aging laboratories and how to structure the most productive research environment.

Information Networking

According to most contemporary pundits, we are entering what is often called the "information age." Although considerable confusion clouds the meaning of this term, we could perhaps identify the information age as one in which a national capacity for selectively preserving, assessing, and effectively using information has achieved a new level of strategic importance. Information has always been critical both to human progress and to the capacity of individual societies to establish leadership in economic, cultural, social, and military matters, but the strategic centrality of massive amounts of information today seems qualitatively different from its position in earlier times.

Since we are in the information age, we have, of course, developed an appropriate science of information and, to add to it, I want to announce two new theorems:

- *Shapiro's Information Science Theorem 1:* "The human capacity to accumulate useless information is unbounded."
- *Shapiro's Information Science Theorem 2* (the theorem of information entropy): "There is an unbounded human capacity to disorder information."

An excellent example of the second theorem is a miscatalogued book, which renders a perfectly good source of information, for all practical purposes, useless. Another example is the promiscuous gathering of information from military satellites without the capacity to distinguish, in a timely fashion, the useful from the useless. Hence, much of what is gathered, even that portion of it which might have been helpful, remains untapped. In my more pessimistic moments, I feel that our tendency to disorder information (that is, make it useless) is slowly approaching our capacity to generate new information. In any case, we clearly collect a great deal more information than we use. There are a number of explanations for this trend: we are not selective enough in what we collect and preserve; it is difficult to forecast future information needs; and we do not preserve our information in a manner that enables us to assess it meaningfully.

One of the great challenges of the age is to defend against the operation of my two theorems—particularly the "information entropy" theorem. We must confront the paradox of why the information age keeps us so poorly informed. As T. S. Eliot asked over fifty years ago, "Where is the knowledge we have lost in information?" It is possible to be more informed and less aware.

Many special characteristics of our era make information ever more crucial. Among these are:

1. *Information pervasiveness:* The strategic importance of information now pervades almost all aspects of our national effort.
2. *Information volume:* The amount of information about us seems almost Himalayan in proportions.
3. *Information change:* The nature of information, like our entire knowledge base, is rapidly changing.
4. *Internationalization:* Societies are more and more interdependent not only in information flows but in cultural, social, economic, and military affairs.

Each of these special characteristics presents a whole new set of challenges for our information system. But this short note will focus only on the internationalization of information.

Today no individual, library, university, institution, region, or country—whether in the world of scholarship or the world of production—is self-sufficient in regard to information. This basic premise implies that effective networking of information is a requirement of our times, if we aspire to maximize our creative potential as individuals, institutions, nation-states, and as a world community. There are, however, two major obstacles to the effective networking of information, especially on an international basis: our ability to understand the goals of information networking and our willingness actually to network information among ourselves. I will treat these obstacles sequentially.

It is tempting to allow ourselves to remain preoccupied only with the formidable logistics of an information system. But without a carefully articulated set of goals, modern technology and information are simply unrealized potentialities. We must develop a capacity to ask the right questions about our information system. To do that, we must understand why we are networking our information in the first place.

The second obstacle is our unwillingness to enter into international networking projects—a much more serious problem than we usually assume. A wave of parochial sentiment and protectionism has recently been sweeping the world community. Some of these new feelings are understandable in light of the enormous changes and challenges that are confronting societies around the world. The institutions we have developed over the last century may simply be ill designed to cope with a world of such rapid change. In any case, this new nationalism—cultural, economic, political, and military—mitigates our capacity to exchange information on an international basis. New barriers are proposed almost daily to inhibit the free flow of information between countries. This protectionist sentiment ought particularly to concern scholars, whose specialized fields know few meaningful international boundaries, and librarians, with their long history of unreserved access to a common knowledge base.

Another difficulty simply exacerbates the protectionist impulse. Since the world community is composed of nation-states with a wide variety of socioeconomic arrangements, each country has allocated its activities somewhat differently between the public and private sectors. For present purposes it is important to note that work carried on in the public sector by definition generates public goods, which are freely available to anyone wishing access to them. Work carried on in the private sector, however, is either not available to others or available only at a price. Thus free and open international networking *only* of that information existing in the public sector in each country would result in inequitable burden-sharing among the various partners to the arrangement. For example, a country carrying on a large part of its research and development effort in the public sector would be giving away information, while a country that assigns the same activity to the private sector would be giving away nothing but instead selling it at a "market" price. In the long run, of course, those who generate information must be compensated for their investment and for the risks they have incurred. The varying institutional arrangements that produce information in different countries, however, greatly complicate the negotiation of an appropriate system for equitable international exchanges. This is a knotty problem, but once it is recognized, we can begin to approach it step by step.

Finally, information processing is the essence both of scientific and technological change and of the capacity of the world's nations to live together. Effective, ongoing communication is a critical component of any organization that wishes to retain its capacity for continuing innovation, and it forms an increasingly vital aspect of international understanding.

The Importance of the Humanities
in a Technological Age

Most commentators agree that technological developments will continue to play a crucial role in the dynamic evolution of our culture. Since American colleges and universities have become heavily involved in the process of technological innovation and diffusion, the changing role of technology could have major implications for the nature of higher education. It is time, therefore, to reaffirm the basic purposes of higher education, its role in society, and the conditions necessary to its continued success. As we take up this reappraisal, one important question will be what role the liberal arts, and the humanities in particular, should play in an information age that focuses intensely on technology and technical training.

Most contemporary discussions of such issues, even on college campuses, are surprisingly ahistorical. In fact, throughout its long voyage of discovery, humankind has always prominently attended to the great questions of ethics and belief that now fall under the rubric of the humanities. It was only by constructing various canons of belief that particular communities, large and small, found it possible to live cooperatively, control their lives, and exploit their surroundings. As it developed a broader understanding of the physical universe and implemented new technologies, the human community made parallel attempts to devise codes of individual and group behavior and associated institutions. In the early periods, legends, myths, and, later, traditional religions interpreted the origin of both the earth and the life on it. An ethical code of individual and social behavior accompanied these accounts of creation. Thus, science was knit together with moral and social behavior into a single fabric.

From the beginning, technology (a particular set of materials, methods, and machines that controls the application of energy) has been as much a part of this history as philosophy and science. It is simply another dimension of a complex interrelated set of forces that define human culture. That is, the key technologies of a period help specify our concept of human beings in relation to nature. We must, in short, understand the potter's wheel to comprehend the ancient world, Descartes and the mechanical clock to appreciate Western culture in the sixteenth and seventeenth centuries, the steam engine to fathom the nineteenth century, and the computer to grasp the latter part of the twentieth. The new metaphor suggested by the computer, for instance, casts human beings as information processors and all of nature as information to be processed.

Despite the long history of technology, in recent times a considerable and unusually severe tension has arisen between developments in science and technology and our understanding of ourselves as a human community. This chasm between science and the human experience may have opened, in part, because common sense can no longer provide the ultimate insight into the physical universe. Using the microscope, the telescope, and the language of mathematics, modern science can discover and describe phenomena quite beyond the grasp of human experience. Interestingly, just when science began to uncover the hidden secrets of the physical universe, social scientists like Sigmund Freud started to posit hidden, or subconscious, wellsprings for individual and social behavior. Alienated from our own common sense as a way of validating experience and understanding, humankind has quite naturally come to feel estranged from those human values that for many centuries infused our lives with meaning. This estrangement gives a new sense of urgency to our search for an integrated and inspiriting view of the universe. A liberal arts education, especially one emphasizing the humanities, holds great promise for effecting just such an integration.

What Are the Liberal Arts?

Although sometimes confused with one of their components—the humanities—the liberal arts include the natural and social sciences. Together the natural and social sciences and the humanities are known as the liberal arts because of their potential to liberate the human intellect and the human spirit. All the liberal arts share certain values and assumptions. They all accept the basic presupposition of an objective reality, which can be discovered through the

application of reason. All therefore value the primacy of truth, in
lectual integrity, imagination, consistency, coherence, and simp
ity. Given our view of the universe, these values tend to hav
civilizing effect upon human beings, helping us to substitute reas
for instinct and deliberativeness for impetuosity. In so doing, they
help to liberate us from unfounded judgments, parochial understandings, and intemperate convictions.

One way that the liberal arts liberate us is by providing the
means to order and interpret our experience. Our inclination to classify experiences and data—what the poet Wallace Stevens called the
"Blessed rage for order"—is well established, perhaps even deep in
our neural structures. The liberal arts satisfy this powerful human
need by offering us ways to organize our sense experience so that the
world seems more intelligible, more predictable, more hospitable.
According to Jacob Bronowski in *Science and Human Values* (New
York, 1972, pp. 13–14):

> All science is the search for unity in hidden likenesses. . . . The
> scientist looks for order in the appearances of nature by explor-
> ing such likenesses. For order . . . is not there for the mere
> looking. There is no way of pointing a finger or a camera at it;
> order must be discovered and, in a deep sense, it must be cre-
> ated. What we see, as we see it, is mere disorder.

For human beings, all experience is an act of exploration; the humanities and the various sciences offer the most sophisticated tools
we have for the journey.

The sciences and the humanities often differ greatly in their
approaches. Scientists may require chemicals to verify a scientific
law or longitudinal data to validate a social tendency, while poets use
the materials of their own lives. Scientist and poet alike, however,
help us construct and order aspects of a single reality. The fact that
Bach can be analyzed either musically or mathematically illustrates
two points: (1) his genius lends itself to at least a bimodal approach,
and (2) the division of intellectual activity into academic disciplines
merely reflects the human need for order rather than legitimate divi-
sions in reality itself. Bach's work is a unity, which is approached
from different angles at different moments. Thus, science and the

humanities each lend special meaning to separable but not mutually exclusive dimensions of human experience.

A Definition of the Humanities

Certain values and emphases distinguish the humanities from the other liberal arts: self-awareness, the appreciation of beauty, reverence for tradition and texts, an understanding of other cultures and worldviews, and attention to human choices and their consequences. Though the intellectual content and methods of the humanities are remarkable for their variety, these common values run through most Western and many non-Western examples of humanistic inquiry. The humanities can be distinguished from the other liberal arts in several ways.

First, each of them centers on the human individual and the process of knowing rather than simply on the body of knowledge to be acquired, as is often the case in the natural and social sciences. How we come to know—whether it be by deduction, induction, intuition, or divine inspiration—together with the difference such knowledge makes for an individual, is as important to the philosopher or the literary critic as what we know.

Secondly, the humanities explicitly concern themselves with intellectual, moral, and aesthetic values. They pose questions which involve the evaluation of the totality of human experience. Analyses of works of fiction, religious writings, or historical texts help us to examine the crucial value dimension of our lives and actions.

Thirdly, the humanities focus on the human individual and the continuity of the culture out of which human beings have emerged over time. The links that can be forged for each individual with the past and toward the future form essential aspects of the humanities. Neither the sciences, nor the arts, nor the social sciences are as concerned with the setting out of which human experience emerges as are literature, history, and anthropology.

Finally, the humanities place value on purity of language and teach us to prize clarity of thought and expression. Though this concern is not unique to the humanities, the disciplines of literature and philosophy place a singular emphasis on language, regarding it not only as a means to an end but as an end in itself. The text and its interpretation or creation are at the very center of humanistic studies. Taken together, the humanities offer us multiple means of evaluating our experience as individuals, both here and now, and as part of the long stream of human history.

The Value of a Humanistic Education

A balanced education should consist of adequate exposure not only to technical and professional education—which most of us agree substantially enhances our lives and communities—but also to the world of values and intellectual discipline, and to their interrelationship. With this in mind, I believe that the role of the humanities within an undergraduate education is twofold. First, undergraduates should learn something of what society is, how it came to be that way, and how they as individuals relate to the larger human community. Although these issues can be illuminated in a number of ways, study of the humanities sensitizes us to such questions as: What can we learn from our collective past? What do we mean by morality? What is art? How should we be governed? Such queries deal directly with our cultural tradition and values and speak to the possibilities of our humanity. By addressing such questions, an undergraduate education should help us create a broader context for our immediate concerns, whatever they may be. It should strengthen our imagination and enlarge our powers of sympathy for other peoples, other cultures, and other ways of behaving. Within the undergraduate curriculum, it is the humanities that specifically focus on these issues.

Secondly, an undergraduate education should offer students the knowledge and insight that empower them to contribute to civilization. As part of this process, it is crucial for students to learn that the concrete present, in science or society, constitutes but one alternative among many. By understanding that our past, as we perceive it, is but one of the paths we could have followed, we gain the breadth of perspective necessary to build the best possible future for humanity. At the same time, we discern the uniqueness of our own age—which is in part that both our problems and our potential derive from the same source, the great advances in science and technology. We must learn how to employ these powerful new capabilities in the most socially useful way. Thus, undergraduate education must not only develop our technical expertise but relate our experience to the broader human landscape in a way that moves us to a purpose and capacity beyond ourselves. Exposure to the humanities can play a critical part in this process and thus in the experience of all thoughtful people.

Plato believed that, at least for some individuals, education should wrest attention from the transitory world of material objects and turn it toward the more permanent intellectual and spiritual sphere. In *The Republic* he argued that the educated person gains insight into reality from contemplation and, somewhat reluctantly, comes to apply that insight to the everyday world. For Plato, what counted in education were the concepts themselves, not their application.

Today most of us prefer exposure to the material realm of technical and professional education. Indeed, I believe the current revival of public interest in and support for education focuses too narrowly on science and technology. There is a widespread but profoundly misguided notion that revitalizing our national efforts in science and technology will alone enable the United States to regain its economic, social, political, and cultural leadership. But, taking a leaf from Plato's book, I would argue instead that we must learn once again to balance material concerns against the world of values and intellectual discipline, which is best approached through the humanities.

Undergraduate education should, in brief, prepare us not only for a livelihood but for a life. To make a living, we may need to know how to build a bridge, plow a field, treat a disease, play a Neapolitan fifth chord, understand the likely duration of a proton lifetime, manage the demands of a classroom of obstreperous young children, or defend a subtle point of common law. But once we have acquired the knowledge and skills that allow us to earn a living, we still have to decide how and when to apply what we have learned and toward what ends. To ensure that such decisions are made thoughtfully, undergraduate education should foster not only knowledge but judgment, not only diligence but imagination, not only skills but insight.

Studying the humanities can give our lives as a whole a sense of balance and direction. Knowledge of history can hone the imagination; training in philosophy can develop critical judgment; reading literary texts can kindle creativity. Without these qualities, the most advanced technical or professional training in the world will flounder. Those who would succeed with their livelihood must be able to set it within a larger context, looking beyond the immediate to what counts in the longer run. Literature, music, art, and history also pay ample dividends in enjoyment and, perhaps more importantly, in personal renewal. An undergraduate education in the humanities can thus provide a meaning for us in the larger context of our lives.

Given all the problems besetting our world today, teaching and scholarship in the humanities might seem a luxury we can ill afford. Particular social problems may seem too urgent, economic needs too vital, and technological requirements too critical to allow us to dwell on such "ephemeral" matters as human values and their implications for our lives. On the contrary, I believe it is precisely at times like these that the literary, cultural, and philosophical dimensions of undergraduate education become most pressing. Universities must continue to sustain a broad balance and a commitment to all aspects of the human endeavor in their teaching and research programs.

Unfortunately, with funding sources outside the universities continuing to dwindle, it may be increasingly difficult for scholars in the humanities to pursue their research and teaching. Libraries, museums, and historical collections may become less accessible as travel funds shrink; with books and other materials deteriorating, existing archives may become less useful. We must continue to maintain and perhaps expand our libraries. We must continue to cherish our museums and historical collections. Above all, we must continue to value the critical insights, balance, and broad perspective that scholarship in the humanities provides.

The Humanities and Society

Many challenges of contemporary life can benefit greatly from the insights afforded by the humanities. One striking example is the question of how to establish a national agenda that balances the demands of business against the necessities of individuals; the needs for power and energy against the desire to preserve the environment; and the requisites of national defense against the needs of our citizens for food, clothing, education, and health care. To negotiate these conflicting demands requires the clarity of thought and expression, farsightedness, imagination, insight, and critical judgment best honed in humanistic study.

To take a specific example, it is useful to understand the various interrelationships governing federal budget data in order to follow debates on the federal budget. But we must also consider how those data should be used and toward what ends federal resources should be deployed. A thoughtful citizen must clearly grasp the substantive issues involved, along with the value judgments implicit in each possible course of action. In our nonauthoritarian society, the quality of an individual voter's reflections on such complex issues crucially affects the quality of the political process. By forging a link between past and present and by clarifying the value implications of political decisions, the humanities give our citizens the wisdom necessary to hold governmental processes in check. By providing a perspective on decision making, the humanities aid us in distinguishing the tractable from the intractable, the essential from the inessential, as we build our future.

Just as the humanities supply the tools for critical evaluation of our political processes, so the imagination, critical acumen, and sensitivity to human values that we gain from the humanities can also facilitate the analysis of technological change. The startling pace of scientific and technological discovery seems to impose on us a "tyranny of the new," which I believe strains the structure of human societies. Our capacity to absorb such change effectively and creatively seems to be governed by a slower clock. The disparity between these two kinds of pacing makes us uneasy about ourselves and our times. We need relief from the present-mindedness that so often seems to obsess us.

Although technological innovations and the material improvements that accompany them can dramatically enhance our quality of life, they ultimately come into being and achieve their full meaning only through our sense of history, our sense of purpose, our values, and our humanity. In the words of Lewis Mumford: "A community whose life is not irrigated by art and science, by religion and philosophy, day upon day, is a community that exists only half alive."

Though technology was meant, as Jacques Ellul's *Technological Society* reminds us, to serve as a buffer between man and nature, it has, in many ways, acquired a life of its own. Nowhere in the contemporary world is its autonomy more apparent than in the area of nuclear weapons development and associated strategic concerns, where the question of basic human purpose hardly ever seems to arise. Perhaps this situation is inevitable, but technology and its uses should at least in part be guided by precisely those considerations to which the study of the humanities makes us sensitive. As Archibald MacLeish observes, "There is in truth a terror in the world and the arts have heard it as they always do. Under the hum of the miraculous machines and the ceaseless publications of brilliant physicists a silence waits and listens and is heard."

That most salient of late twentieth-century technological breakthroughs—the computer—exemplifies the need for not only sophisticated scientific thought but also subtle humanistic distinctions. Ever since Pascal and Leibniz, people have dreamed of machines that could perform intellectual tasks. It is surprisingly complicated to decide whether or not the computer fulfills this dream. To make the most creative use of this technology, we must confront or at least meaningfully approach such questions as:

- Is the computer a model of human cognition as computation, or is it best understood as a symbol manipulator, or is this a distinction without a difference?
- If the computer is considered a symbol manipulator, can meaningful symbols be manipulated by purely logical operations?
- Is a computer conscious, does it think, does it have a soul or an inner life?
- Why can the computer easily perform tasks that are hard for us yet fail completely at tasks we find easy?

As a moment's reflection will reveal, grappling with these questions requires us to comprehend the role of human beings in relation to nature, understand the values and aspirations of society, and imagine how we can most effectively and meaningfully continue to coexist with our environment. These are matters for which the study of the liberal arts, especially the humanities, best prepares us.

Science and technology by themselves yield few economic, social, or cultural dividends and are clearly not sufficient for the construction of a humane society. What we need in addition is a dynamic and responsive set of economic, social, and political institutions that use science and technology to yield human benefits. In the decades ahead, if we in the United States wish to maintain world leadership, it will not be enough for us simply to possess technological and scientific expertise. We must come to understand that it is only through social cohesion and a set of shared values and commitments that we can sustain the vitality of our human communities. That is why equal opportunity for all our citizens is so important. All of the science and technology in the world alone will never resolve our problems or allow us to exert world leadership without the requisite social institutions and shared values. And, as I have been urging, it is a humanistic education that can best point us toward these larger goals.

Policy and Resource Issues in a Contemporary Democracy

Confronting Reality and Building the Future: Race Relations and the Future of Our Liberal Democracy

One of the most significant, fundamental, and redeeming features of American society is its cultural diversity. It is essential to our common sense of humanity and to America's continued economic and cultural leadership that we successfully realize the potential that our diversity represents. In order to develop this potential, we will have to work toward eliminating those ethnic, religious, and racial prejudices—and the social arrangements associated with them—that continue to impede our achievement of this social and moral goal.

As I see it, however, there is a crisis in our community. We must make certain economic and social changes, and in order to do so, we cannot remain as rigidly constrained by our history as our current rhetoric suggests we are. We must see ourselves not only as capable of action but as capable of new types of action. It is just as debilitating not to conceive new opportunities or pursue those that are open to us as it is to believe that we can operate completely outside the confines of our history and biology. The opportunity for social progress lies somewhere between utopia and paralysis, and it is essential that we begin to define and occupy more of this middle ground.

Democracy depends critically on participation—which is unlikely to occur among those without hope. It is imperative, therefore, that democratic societies not only avoid a sense of fatalism but cultivate all those conditions that ensure a rising sense of hope and possibility throughout the entire community. We cannot allow our disappointing progress to sink us into a crippling pessimism. We must instead remain dedicated to the idea of eventual deliverance from suffering and oppression, which is one of the great themes of Western political thought. And we must understand that this commitment requires a profound strength of purpose and discipline as well as a constant readiness to embrace the best options available. We must all recognize that continuous compromise and reconciliation of diverse interests are fundamental components of a liberal democracy.

We can be justly proud of the achievements of American democracy and of the institutions and values that structure our society. But we must at the same time acknowledge that the benefits of these achievements have not been equally shared by every group in our increasingly diverse society, particularly not by the significant portion of our population that is Black. Despite considerable progress in this area in recent decades, racism in its various forms continues to place an intolerable burden on many of our fellow citizens.

This continuing racism, along with a heritage of slavery, has created the framework within which the Afro-American culture, a distinctly American phenomenon, has been forged. Thus, for a variety of complex reasons, current and historical social arrangements have resulted in an immigrant experience for Blacks that differs importantly from that of other ethnic groups. These factors have also led to the underrepresentation of Blacks in positions of power and prestige to a degree that cannot be explained by differences—if any—in personal preferences and/or human capacity. Unquestionably, the guardians of our political, economic, and judicial systems have found effective means to block the full participation of Blacks, thus allowing the Black community to suffer unique levels of social deprivation and inequality. What may be less well understood is how the resultant survival strategies adopted by Black communities have fundamentally shaped Afro-American culture and how they influence the possibilities for our joint future.

An important impediment to this understanding may be our rhetoric. Although racism has led to difficulties we must now address, we seem to have reached the point where charging an individual or group with racism too often substitutes for thoughtful and progressive action on all parts. At times the emotional impact of our vocabulary—especially when its bent is rhetorical rather than conversational—can overwhelm its descriptive and analytic power. In such cases, the rhetoric itself may inhibit action, obstructing thoughtful discussion and progress on pressing social issues. When words lose their meaning, there is always a greater loss, since language is intrinsic to effective communication and mutual under-standing. We are especially prone to this loss when we use single words or phrases to represent what are, in reality, deep and complex problems.

The term "racism," like the term "holocaust," has been so encumbered with emotion and overuse as to severely limit its effi-cacy, except for the rhetorical arousal of emotion and the understand-able ventilation of deep anger and frustration. Similarly, little has been gained by attributing to "institutional racism" all the remain-ing undesirable outcomes not ascribed to "personal racism." In pub-lic debate, defining a person, group, institution, or issue as "racist" may give rise to passion and guilt, but it seldom elicits a commit-ment to change, and it is a changed world that we need.

Unfortunately, the contemporary rhetoric of racism often casts both Blacks and whites as victims and thus leads to a community-wide paralysis of will. In this framework, both Blacks and whites view whites as the victims of inherited prejudices and special privi-leges, which prevent them from understanding the issues and/or wanting to change and therefore from undertaking any new initia-tives in race relations. Blacks, on the other hand, are perceived as the victims of a history of oppression that undermines their capacity to realize their human potential more fully. I believe there is a mortal danger to any community that views itself as powerless to influence its own circumstances. If *both* Blacks and whites are perceived as helpless victims of racism, it seems futile to consider new initia-tives. In short, the rhetoric of racism may have fixated us on only part of the truth. It may be serving less to illuminate the present than to confuse our potential future with certain aspects of our history and to deflect our attention from what we need most: community-wide initiatives that can create a better future for us all.

Improvement in race relations will require that white and Black communities move toward each other. Because of the salient cultural differences between these communities, we cannot easily follow the path taken by many white ethnic groups, which eagerly shed certain aspects of their own cultures in exchange for the oppor-tunity to join the mainstream. Although accommodation and assimi-lation of different cultures has been a hallmark of American history, I believe that the uniqueness of the Black experience in America may call for certain strategies and objectives that were not considered and/or desired by other ethnic communities in America. We must, therefore, think harder about our past and the particularity of the Black experience in America in order to envision a future for us all that is both plausible and compelling.

As we try realistically to construct a better future in race relations, we must not ignore or wish away the long-established tendency of most human communities to gather together in discrete groups. Ethnocentrism has always been a part of human societies. People have historically congregated in groups both for their mutual sustenance and for the expression of their human spirit. Furthermore, groups have always adopted a set of rules about who belongs (and thus has certain obligations and rights) and who does not. It is crucial to the survival of any particular group that its members rely on and sustain one another. These bonds of affection, caring, and commitment may or may not inhere genetically (i.e., be driven by the process of natural selection and differential gene replication) in the human species, but they are clearly essential for the survival of human communities. At the same time, however, these self-nourishing communities often also exhibit an astonishing, frightening, and outrageous capacity for cruelty toward those perceived as outsiders. Sadly, groups often assert the primacy of their own outlook, values, and place in the evolving culture through aggressive behavior toward others. Although racism can be viewed, in part, as a special case of ethnocentrism, distinctions based on color have proved especially pernicious to the human spirit of the entire community. In addition, as already noted, racism in America has created a distinct culture that requires special and distinct responses.

In the modern world, different ethnic and cultural groups have many more opportunities for contact than they did a century or even a few decades ago. It is, however, difficult to assess whether these opportunities enhance or reduce the potential for intergroup harmony. On the one hand, more frequent interaction could promote greater understanding and less fear, but much of contemporary communication is progressively more specialized and impersonal. Thus, while we increasingly find ourselves in a "common cauldron," genuine human communication is more difficult and rarer than ever. In addition, more contact between dissimilar groups makes differences difficult to ignore and may create a greater need to assert our own sense of values and identification. We must try to handle the conflicts engendered by this situation in a nondestructive, even productive way. If we succeed, we will have solved the great mystery of how different cultures can work together without constructing a social and economic environment that assigns some groups to a "natural" second-class status.

One of the most redeeming aspects of our society's liberal institutions is their basis in the idea that different groups should be able to get along together (i.e., have common access to procedural justice) without completely agreeing on what is good, just, and worthy. In addition, throughout American history different groups have tended gradually to expand their notions of just who belongs to their community and is therefore fully entitled to the privileges of membership. At the same time, however, the expansion of sensitivities across racial lines has been excruciatingly slow. Moreover, pluralism, the companion idea of our liberal institutions, is based on the notion that different races, cultures, or ethnicities can peacefully—even productively—coexist by celebrating their variation. Pluralism validates cultural diversity and requires that we mediate our cultural and other conflicts through various nondestructive mechanisms. There must, of course, be some common values (e.g., a commitment to pluralism) for this to work. Without a binding set of common values, a coherent society is impossible.

Pluralism may be one of the most daring experiments in human history. At this point, however, we must ask whether the liberal institutions of our pluralistic society can continue enlarging the reciprocal sympathies of our various constituent groups until they have all been completely integrated into our system of justice and our spectrum of opportunities. Only if further progress is possible in this arena can we hope to sustain essential intergroup harmony. The great calling of liberal societies, it seems to me, is not to make one group from many, but to build from many varying cultural, racial, and ethnic groups a federation of diversity in which we share some key concepts. Although human beings will never all belong to a single group, it may be possible for us to live productively together. Such, in any case, is the aim of Western liberalism and pluralism.

The opposite of pluralism, fundamentalism (in its various guises), proclaims the superiority of one particular culture, often citing a special source for its revelation. Rather than celebrate the free play of ideas, fundamentalism—like other extreme ideologies—

deplores dissent as a barrier to the achievement of some cultural utopia. The great challenge for a liberal/pluralistic society is to sustain a morally energizing vision of its prospects while forgoing utopian tactics. Realizing this goal will also require responsibility, self-discipline, and, above all, a commitment to human reciprocity and community needs. While we must certainly stand for something (or we will fall for anything), we must also constantly encourage critical evaluation of new alternatives. We attempt this delicate balancing act in the name of a truly equitable, just, and inspiring future. Without a compelling vision, freedom to choose is almost a waste.

Attempting to sustain a culturally diverse community within the context of a just and equitable society generates other challenges as well. History yields striking evidence of the social and cultural fragility of societies that are not bound together by a dominant religious goal, a particular political crusade, or a strong kinship tradition. In America, we have increasingly identified the individual as the ultimate source of values and meaning, relying on the institutions of liberal justice to link us all together. The challenge of maintaining such a system is heightened by the current ascendancy of individualism: kinship associations are breaking down, truly personal communication is diminishing, dominant social forms vest individuals with ever greater autonomy, and modern ideology and technology seem to promise limitless possibilities for individual development. We appear to have almost lost our understanding that we realize our individuality through others. Our liberal/pluralistic approach will always require us to weigh these escalating individual liberties against group and community needs.

Despite its many failures and the increasing contradiction between modern technology and social cohesion, the United States has been unusually successful in accommodating and benefiting from diversity. Indeed, the fact that new immigrant groups expected to feel "at home" in a new country is a distinctly American phenomenon. Yet our aspirations are far from fulfilled, and we now confront a moment in history when our unifying moral and political commitments are deteriorating, and when our obsession with expanding individual freedoms outruns our concern for their appropriate use. While our ethnic and racial diversity is increasing, some groups are neither faring well nor experiencing equitable treatment. Large segments of our society continue to be excluded from the full range of educational, economic, social, and judicial opportunities. The statistics of hardship in urban Black communities and much of rural America are especially grievous. Much current discussion focuses on who should be responsible for ameliorating this situation: the family; the excluded or partially excluded group itself; various federal, social, and economic policies; or the majority groups that are refusing fully to share the keys to opportunity. Underlying this contemporary debate is the continued but dimly understood effect of our long and difficult social history. An important question for our future is whether the liberal institutions of our society can continue to alter social arrangements in a manner consistent with both individual freedoms and our need to develop the full potential of our cultural and social diversity.

In my work as president of a major research university, I have experienced firsthand the difficulties that people of goodwill—both Black and white—face in trying to alleviate longstanding and painful inequities in educational opportunity and achievement. The integration of schools, the opening up of universities, antipoverty programs, and other civil rights and Great Society initiatives have not yielded the full results we anticipated. Affirmative action—originally proposed as a temporary remedy—now seems likely to be with us for the indefinite future since fundamental inequalities have not diminished nearly as rapidly as we had thought they might. We now appreciate that problems of race and poverty, which we once thought would succumb to traditional political and economic solutions, have historical, psychological, motivational, and cultural dimensions that continue to elude us.

As in other areas, however, our rhetoric more often serves as a barrier than as a productive stimulus to genuine communication and understanding. Rather than focusing on needed changes in both the Black and white communities, we have too often expended energy denouncing one another's motives, values, decency, and humaneness. If these hyperbolic denunciations were the whole truth, we would be a country without hope or demonstrated achievement. Our rhetoric has prevented us—Blacks and whites—from joining together and realistically assessing the problems before us.

Lasting progress will require a more honest articulation of the problems we face, even when they raise highly sensitive issues. It will also require new relationships based on trust, the courage to explore new solutions to complex problems, and a capacity for constructive dialogue. Currently, few of us can even accept honest criticism. The problems we confront are far deeper and more complex than can be explained by either a "lack of will" among Blacks or racism on the part of whites. New initiatives are desperately needed to sustain the progress we have made and propel us to even greater strides in the future. We must learn to approach this issue as a common project designed to redeem us all.

In my view, cultural diversity is an inherently valuable and probably enduring characteristic of our society. Since we are unlikely to arrive at a common idea of what is just, beautiful, right, holy, or worthy, our moral worth depends upon a toleration of diversity. Furthermore, as much of modern Western history has demonstrated, cultural and intellectual pluralism promote a valuable tendency toward social innovation. The cost, of course, of this tendency is a restless anxiety, which is one of the prices we pay for progress and which may be a permanent feature of an increasingly diverse society. We gain nothing by pretending otherwise. On the other hand, we may gain a great deal by acknowledging this diversity, recognizing the potential for both conflict and human growth in such an environment, and designing nonviolent and productive means for resolving social, economic, and political disputes. Such an acknowledgment focuses attention on the real issues and, more importantly, provides a framework that impels us to action. We perceive ourselves as moral agents with opportunities and obligations rather than as helpless victims of the past.

Obviously, many economic and social problems still burden certain racial groups more than others. But we must be able to look beyond—although not past—simple racial explanations in order to generate useful new courses of action. Such problems as equal opportunity, cultural diversity, teenage pregnancy, single-parent households, substance abuse, and adequate nutrition are not usefully addressed purely as racial problems any more than low farm prices are usefully considered elements in a war against rural America. It is only when we assess these issues in their broader historical and social context that we may discover the beginnings of a solution.

Finally, in a modern, culturally diverse, mobile society, government *must* play a crucial role in enabling all groups to work together and ensuring more equal opportunities for all. To achieve this end, it must mobilize resources and provide moral leadership. In this sense, our government should be viewed as an extension of our own individual aspirations and needs. In contemporary America, government initiatives are required, for example, to help us address the calamity of children in poverty as well as the economic and social disintegration of some of our once-great cities. We need government initiatives to ensure that certain individuals and institutions will mediate between those in distress and those who enjoy a broad range of opportunities. In those desperate parts of our great country that are currently without hope, the government must help create conditions in which hope can once again arise.

The liberation of us all requires substantially increased assistance to those of us in need, and government initiatives are one of the essential ways we can work together to achieve this end. Market mechanisms are not always adequate to mobilize society's resources for certain objectives. I understand the limitations of government initiatives, the chasm that often separates the good intentions of legislatures from the realization of these intentions through actual public programs. Still, we cannot allow past failures or successes to blind us to future possibilities. Each of us must work individually and in private groups, and all of us must support appropriate government policies. The tragedy of certain trends in public policy is that this critical role of government is being abdicated through budget policies and tax reforms that focus on economic efficiency alone. In a genuinely progressive society, moral and social imperatives must be addressed by government as well as the private sector. Indeed, it is these imperatives that undergird our future prosperity.

Are Schools for Learning?

During my youth in the 1930s and 1940s, the white middle class shared a strong consensus about the function of schools and the values they were to teach. We believed that schools were of course for learning and, even more importantly, they were primarily for learning. By "learning" we normally meant not only academic achievement (the development of knowledge and cognitive skills), but also the acquisition of the chief tenets of the Western cultural tradition.

In those years we focused little attention on the insensitivity of the schools to the needs of the more vulnerable or disadvantaged children in our society. There was a general commitment to equality of educational opportunity, but we did not always think carefully about it. Today's concerns with equality of access, equality of treatment, and the overall equality of life chances remained a largely unarticulated aspect of public policy, reserved for the farther reaches of our social conscience. Differences in cognitive skills and achievement were accepted as real phenomena and, moreover, constituted an acceptable moral justification for improving the life chances of a particular individual. In recent decades, however, we have witnessed the emergence of new ideas concerning achievement and equality, ideas that have important implications for our schools.

The United States has always been subject to social change and its attendant tensions—occasionally erupting into civil war or riots—as we have tried to balance our commitments to liberty, equality, progress, justice, and economic well-being. Until our own time, we seem, with some notable lapses, to have managed these forces of change relatively well. In fact, for generations "change" was synonymous with "progress" in the American consciousness, despite the inevitable strain it placed on existing social institutions and their practices. As the pace of change has accelerated and become less predictable, however, the potential for conflict among various groups in our society has increased, taxing both the capacities of our institutions to reconcile competing interests *and* the willingness of special interest groups to accept any compromise. American society, as we know it, is absolutely dependent on the vitality of our integrative institutions and processes, which enable us to achieve workable compromises. The American public school system has been a leading example of such an integrative process, and it should not surprise us that it now shows signs of considerable stress.

Unfortunately, in the last decade the power and influence of many of our society's major integrative institutions have declined. This process parallels a diminishing faith in traditional values and the associated weakening of all kinds of authority. What has emerged in their place are a fragmented social dictatorship exercised by special interest groups and an uneasy moral relativism. As one result, we are less confident of our ability to make moral distinctions. We are less able to classify acts as moral or immoral, and less able to decide on the appropriate use of authority.

Our schools have been a crucial social institution throughout American history and, like other institutions, their role responds to changes in our cultural outlook and has thus shifted over time. In our contemporary search for "progress," we may have looked to our schools to fill certain roles for which they were unprepared, perhaps even unsuited, and thus undermined what I believe ought to remain their primary purpose: that is, constantly raising the level of scholastic achievement. Such an ideal is necessary because in a vibrant and developing society such as ours, the average level of student achievement must, at very least, grow along with other societal goals. We should be no more content with a stable level of scholastic achievement than with a stable standard of living. Stability in either of these areas will unnecessarily inhibit our creative potential and make it impossible to address the unfinished business on our social agenda. For example, to be useful, the definition of functional literacy must be more demanding now than it was at the turn of the century. There is no indication that we have yet approached the limits of our students' cerebral capacity.

Like many other observers of contemporary American life, I am disheartened by the seemingly meager achievements of our educational system and, increasingly, by evidence of faltering public support for and understanding of the overall enterprise. This essay, then, summarizes my own *selective* assessment of the current status of schooling in the United States. It is not designed to be well balanced or even fair, but to focus instead on a particular set of issues, even at the risk of seeming insensitive to certain responsibilities and genuine continuing accomplishments of our schools. As an outsider, I am acutely conscious of the Spanish proverb: "It is not the same to talk of bulls as to be in the bull ring." On the other hand, the flight of the bird allows a viewpoint not easily available to those on the ground.

A number of simple observations can be made about the resources we presently devote to the central element in our education system, the public elementary and secondary schools.

1. We spend more per capita and per student than any other industrialized nation, even when adjusted for our overall standard of living (i.e., level of real wages).
2. We keep more students in school for longer periods of time than any other industrialized nation.
3. Our teachers have more formal training (in years of schooling) than anywhere else.
4. The resources committed to this area are more evenly distributed here than in other industrialized countries.
5. Our resource commitment to elementary and secondary schools, on a per-pupil basis, has grown over twice as fast as growth in our national income, and in the last two decades student/faculty ratios have fallen by 30 percent. Regardless of whether our resource commitment is sufficient, it has been growing both absolutely and in relation to our national wealth.

Thus, we are first among the world's nations in the commitment of resources to education. Yet we do not rank first in intellectual achievement. This apparent paradox has attracted the interest and concern of many observers. Although the evidence is inconclusive and even somewhat controversial, comparative studies (sponsored first by the United Nations Educational, Scientific, and Cultural Organization and later by the International Education Association) seem to rank our graduates well below those of many other nations in most of the standard academic disciplines. Moreover, this overall assessment remains basically unaffected by correcting the data for the percentage of young people graduated.

Both international and domestic evidence clearly indicate a weak relationship between resource commitments and specific academic achievements. Equally disturbing, no substantial evidence suggests that the overall performance of our schools, especially in the higher grades, is improving, despite—until very recently— increasing resource commitments. Indeed, certain areas seem to be deteriorating, even in an absolute sense. The only bright spot is the evidence pointing to the positive impact of national efforts in reading and mathematics at the elementary school (to grade five) level.

Our elementary and secondary school systems can, of course, provide other valuable learning experiences besides intellectual achievement. They can, for example, impart standards of judgment (values) concerning the major areas of human endeavor, teach vocational skills, or stimulate an interest in and capacity for continued learning. While it is more difficult to evaluate our successes in these areas, the evidence is not reassuring.

In perhaps their most important success of recent decades, however, the nation's schools have made great strides on the issue of access. They deserve particular praise for this achievement because, on a per-student basis, each successive cohort of school-age population is more and more expensive to incorporate into the "mainstream." This expense can be ascribed both to the strain on existing facilities and personnel and to the educationally more deprived background from which the successive cohorts normally come. Unfortunately, this period of increased access has not been marked by any noticeable increase in productivity (i.e., introduction of effective, but efficient, new techniques).

One thing is clear: we no longer seem to share or enthusiastically support a coherent vision of the role schools should play in our society. In part, this is because educational leaders have not provided us with one. The main problem, I believe, is that the de facto role of our schools has come to be considerably broader and more complex than to stimulate academic achievement. These shifting commitments have been disastrous for the schools, for the students, and for our society.

It is not surprising that our schools have changed significantly in the last decades, since they both form and reflect many salient characteristics of the society within which they function. Lamentably, public attention has often concentrated on the wrong dimensions of change. The attention of policymakers and other opinion leaders has converged almost exclusively on the various organizational matters that have so badly fragmented the governance of our schools: the consolidation of school districts, loss of local control, the impact of collective bargaining, methods of finance, the increased role of state and federal government, and the controversial role of the courts. All these issues are worthy of discussion and probably influence the overall achievement levels of the students in our schools, but in my judgment, we should have primarily focused our attention on other issues: declines in reading comprehension, proliferation of nonacademic subjects, the classroom and home climate, and the amount and quality of instruction and instructors.

Equally important is a series of broader ideological and attitudinal shifts regarding social arrangements in this country. Since these shifts set the framework within which schools operate, we must consider them as we assess the performance of our schools and outline a vision of their future. Chief among them are the social relations of authority, both in and beyond the family.

With respect to education, we have recently found ourselves less comfortable with ascribing authority to parents over children, teachers over students, administrators over teachers, judges over administrators. Perhaps one of the most striking changes has been in our attitude toward children. We have begun to strip away the role of both the parent and the school in setting boundaries and values that could guide the social, cognitive, and moral development of children. Most significantly, we have systematically stripped the school and the teacher of their social authority. A new equality between adults and children has been declared, despite the testimony of millennia pointing to the obvious differences in both experience and levels of dependence. Both family and school have been put on the defensive, almost as if we had been systematically exploiting our children throughout our previous history. We take seriously the idea of schools as "instruments of oppression." Unfortunately, this ideological pressure has been reinforced by other contemporary social pressures, especially shifting family patterns.

Rising divorce rates, more single-parent families, more reconstituted families, increased parental absence from the two-job household, unavailable grandparents, later child rearing, smaller families—these developments have been driven, among other forces, by what some contemporary writers suggest is the growing egocentrism, narcissism, and romanticism of purely personal ideologies. The decision to bear children at times seems less motivated by personal and social responsibility than by a wish for a "deep human experience." Is it any surprise, then, that we have forgotten the crucial role of the family in helping to develop the creative potential, social as well as individual, of the next generation? Compassion, no matter how well intentioned, is no substitute for the guidance required to ensure a child's intellectual and personal growth. We have neglected to tell our children that if they enjoy greater choice and independence now, they may endure a lifetime of greater dependence. Henry James's depiction of Isabel Archer in *Portrait of a Lady* sensitively represents the tensions many Americans feel between the attractions of self-indulgence and the need for self-control.

We have failed to address honestly the question of whether contemporary family styles can provide the nurturance, the protection, the social stimulation, and the ultimate freedom necessary to a child's optimal social and cognitive development. Some changes in the relationship between parents and children are undoubtedly desirable. Nevertheless, current research indicates that children from single-parent or changing families have lower achievement rates and more behavior problems than other students, and such problems affect not only the individual child but that child's entire classroom. If our schools are to succeed, we must candidly evaluate the impact of new family forms on the cognitive and emotional development of children.

In the last decades, then, our schools have sought to accommodate students with increasingly diverse cultural and family backgrounds and a range of sometimes irreconcilable interests. We have succeeded in bringing all these groups into the high school, but in the process have lost track of any unifying purpose for keeping them there. Indeed, it is this very diversity that is partially responsible for the collapse of the core curriculum. Today's schools reflect a social vision of a mosaic rather than a melting pot. We must remember, however, that our pluralism and heterogeneity are a source of great strength and creativity only if we maintain strong bonds of affinity, sympathy, and interaction with one another. A melting pot that produced a uniform substance would not be an exciting prospect, but neither would a mosaic with impermeable boundaries.

We will have to decide whether our increased commitment to heterogeneity in personal and social arrangements supports our inherited vision of a democratic and pluralistic society or whether such a commitment threatens what I believe to be the primary goals of our educational system. At very least, responding to this new social vision may demand great changes in our schools. One strategy would be to assume the breakdown of a social consensus and design our schools to respond to the growing differentiation of lifestyles and individual desires. But such a plan may undermine both our schools as centers of intellectual achievement and our concept of an integrative, pluralistic democracy. In this context, the various voucher proposals, economically efficient as they may be, further endanger our capacity to sustain a broad set of social institutions and the common value system that must be their foundation. As Walter Lippmann has observed, we can hardly be expected to be a community if we do not share some knowledge, some faith, or some body of moral and intellectual principles.

In our confused responses to recent social change, we have above all, it seems to me, forgotten that the only standard of performance that can sustain a democracy dedicated to equal opportunity is actual achievement. Instead, we have told a generation of students that intellectual achievement is unrelated to their progress through our school systems. Social adjustment, individual realization, and group consciousness are currently valued at least as highly as achievement is. We have, in the end, exploited our students and fooled ourselves. We have assured them that society would lower both the external and internal barriers to their progress when, in fact, our control was largely limited to the external barriers to individual progress. As a result, we have invested too little in them and in our country's future.

It is not the teachers who are primarily to blame for this unsatisfactory state of affairs in our schools, although many professional organizations (e.g., unions, schools of education, accrediting bodies) must shoulder their share of the responsibility. As Ernest Boyer has so effectively pointed out, we pay far more attention to the importance of education than we do to its primary producers—the teachers. The schools continue to retain many dedicated individuals despite some misguided personnel policies. For teachers, as for students, achievement, not seniority, ought to be the measure of progress.

Rather than teachers, key educational leaders at all levels should be faulted for their lack of guidance and understanding. Schools cannot simply mirror the society they serve; education is too difficult and too complex for that. The open classroom as an idealized image of society was bound to fail as a general model. It is not wishful thinking, but hard thinking about specific attainable goals that pays off. We must decide, once again, that schools are for learning.

We are completing some years of great frustration with our schools, but our vision must be stronger than our frustrations. This is only possible if our vision is clear and if it is consistent with the needs and aspirations of our society. Much has changed in our society, and our schools must, of course, respond. If, however, we are going to enhance our creative potential for leadership in the decades ahead, the schools must react by asserting the absolute requirement of intellectual achievement for *all* students.

Our investment in our children and their education, unlike other investments, is not something that we own; it is a gift to them and to our society's future. Such an investment, however, makes meaningful our own contributions to contemporary life. We should not hesitate to support our schools fully as centers of learning and as our hope for the future. This time, however, let us not burden our schools with yet another round of changed expectations without also committing ourselves to the process for the long term.

In preparing this essay, I have benefited from discussions with Bernard J. Shapiro, Director, Ontario Institute for Studies in Education. He is, however, not implicated in any of the proposals or conclusions contained herein.

Philanthropy: Tradition and Change

Philanthropy and philanthropic organizations have a venerable history, which can put in perspective the contemporary efforts of granting agencies and charitable foundations to sort out their mission. The concepts of charity and philanthropy lie at the very root of Western civilization. The word *philanthropy* itself derives from the Greek *philanthropia*, meaning "love of humanity." The word *charity* evolved from the Latin *caritas*, meaning "affection."

As reflected in the classical languages of our civilization, these concepts indicate an early understanding and appreciation in Western cultures of the bonds that we believe link all of humankind. Indeed, this notion that bonds link all of humankind is, in my judgment, a distinguishing aspect of Western culture. I use the word *bond* advisedly as it has, in this context, a critical double meaning. It constitutes a positive emotional connection among people, but it also (as in *bondage*) constrains them, making them responsible for one another. The earliest concepts of charity and philanthropy, therefore, reflect a sense of reaching out to those in need, not only to help them but also to further the realization of our own humanity.

Cicero once noted that "In nothing do men more nearly approach the gods than in doing good for their fellow men." The old Hebrew proverb "Charity is the spice of riches," while almost hedonistic, speaks directly to the gratification that the philanthropist feels. Nor is the concept of charity limited to Western cultures. When a disciple asked Confucius for a definition of charity, the master answered, "Love one another."

At its roots charity may be defined as the tangible expression of concern toward those individuals or institutions to whom one does not have specific legal obligations. A further distinction can be made between two parallel forms of beneficence that developed over time. The first, initially an outgrowth of the Judeo-Christian tradition, extended help to the sick, the hungry, or the needy. Religious teachings, such as the biblical injunction to love one's neighbor, helped to build and reinforce such behavior.

Among the Greeks and Romans, however, there developed another form of charity based on the general notion of civic responsibility. Rather than directly relieving the suffering of particular individuals, this type of giving focused on enriching public life through the support of particular institutions. Although the separation between these two concepts has never been absolute, this second kind of charity has become an increasingly important aspect of modern philanthropy. Ultimately, of course, all forms of charity and philanthropy directly or indirectly extend far beyond the requirements of particular individuals or groups, encompassing the needs and expressing the aspirations of society at large.

One of the most famous Greek philanthropists was Plato, who founded his Academy in 387 B.C. and dedicated it to educating the young people of Athens. Since at that time there was no means for the Academy to acquire independent legal or financial status, Plato bequeathed his institution and some fertile land around it to a nephew, who was charged with administering it for the good of Plato's students.

Following Plato's example, a series of prominent Greek citizens donated theaters, stadiums, and aqueducts to the various cities in which they resided. The Romans, always in the forefront of legal developments, noted a gap in their own law concerning such donations and set about making it possible for charitable organizations to exist in perpetuity. The modern foundation, with its structural similarity to the corporation, can trace its legal ancestry, then, to changes in Roman law occurring as early as 150 B.C.

In addition to Greek civic ideals and the enabling effect of Roman legislation, religious teachings continued to play a major role in the development of modern philanthropy. During the Middle Ages the Catholic Church's admonition to its adherents to be Good Samaritans resulted in the accumulation of vast financial resources, which were administered through ecclesiastical foundations.

Whereas the early Church had often viewed charity as a temporary remedy for individual failings, during and after the Protestant Reformation poverty began to be seen as resulting from social as well as individual conditions. People came to believe that attacking the underlying social causes of poverty, stress, and deprivation might be a way to complement, although never completely replace, giving to individuals in desperate need.

As political power passed from ecclesiastical to secular hands in the early modern era, the source of charitable giving shifted from a single, central institution to many decentralized, private, foundation-like organizations. Charitable societies, guilds, and fraternal bodies grew and thrived. As in many other cases, this change in social and political institutions can be traced to changes in beliefs and attitudes.

Under Elizabeth I, the Statute of Charitable Uses was enacted in 1601. This statute demonstrated the dual role of a charitable trust as partly private and partly public. Representing society's interest in the work of charitable trusts, the state insisted on playing a role in their formation. This role is still evident today in the charters of charitable foundations, in their structures, their tax exemptions, and the public responsibilities that the law requires of them.

Philanthropy in the United States

When philanthropy reached the United States, it took on a uniquely American character. American charities showed, for example, a more practical bent than their European counterparts. One of the first well-known philanthropists in the New World was Benjamin Franklin, who set aside funds for public works "of the most general utility." After accumulating for 115 years, the funds were sufficient to build and equip the Franklin Institute in Boston. James Smithson, a British scientist, bequeathed $500,000 to the U.S. government, which it used to establish the Smithsonian Institution. The purpose of the Smithsonian was, and is, "the increase and diffusion of knowledge among men."

The form of philanthropy these endowments represent encapsulates, in a distinctly American way, the goal of enhancing the general welfare. There are many such examples. In 1867 George Peabody established the Peabody Education Fund to help rehabilitate the South after the Civil War. Around the turn of the century, Andrew Carnegie and John D. Rockefeller turned their attention and immense resources to the search for ways to improve the human condition. The Guggenheims, Dukes, and Hartfords made similar commitments. By

1910 establishing hospitals, libraries, and foundation-supported research programs had become a major philanthropic activity in the United States.

American attitudes toward the appropriate roles of the public and private sectors also had a shaping influence on American philanthropy. In 1913 the contributions of the Carnegie Corporation to the cause of education exceeded that of the federal government. Philanthropy in the United States incorporated the uniquely American ideas of voluntary action and decentralization of responsibility in the service of society. Indeed, the granting of tax deductions for charitable gifts typifies this decentralization of initiative.

American philanthropy played another particularly crucial role during the culminating century of the great Industrial Revolution (1850–1950), a time when the "free market" ideology of capitalism was in the ascendant. The Industrial Revolution liberated enormous creative energies in our society and is largely responsible for the great wealth we enjoy today. In the name of the great new political and economic freedoms of the time, however, we abandoned the authority of the emperor, the Church, and the family, replacing them with the new "nation-state" and the concept of individual responsibility.

Unfortunately, this environment fostered a growing sense of individual shame about dependency on others. We found ourselves returning to an earlier analysis of individual need as an indication of personal failure. To their great credit, many American philanthropists of this period took a longer, more thoughtful view of the situation. Hence their philanthropy helped fulfill the human potential of the Industrial Revolution.

Philanthropy and the Future of Michigan

The tradition of philanthropy, particularly the establishment of philanthropic foundations, was as strong in Michigan as anywhere else in the country. The names of the great Michigan foundations— Kellogg, Ford, Kresge, Mott, Dow, and many others—have permanently enriched not only the life of this region but also the prospects for humanity in general.

What new mission will be appropriate for philanthropy in the future? Since philanthropy acts in response to social problems, how might it best respond to the problems currently facing our society? In this respect we should recall the words of the Elizabethan statesman and scholar Francis Bacon: "He that will not apply new remedies must expect new evils."

As history amply testifies, the methods and objectives of social institutions must change to meet changing times. Philanthropy has increased its purview from acts of individual charity to the complex but decentralized network of foundations, big and small, that today enhances American life.

Each generation discovers new dimensions to the ancient notion of charity. As we come to understand more about the nature of human society, we deepen our insight into the fundamentally human question of how benevolence might best be expressed. It is thus inevitable that the answers and methods devised by the benefactors of the past will seem insufficient to the problems of today. The challenges of change affect not only philanthropic foundations but all major institutions in society. Indeed change is the absolute prerequisite of creative and effective participation in a dynamic world.

From a worldwide perspective, the outstanding realities of our time are the widespread existence of operational nuclear weapons, on the one hand, and the need to nourish and improve life for our rapidly growing and increasingly dense population, on the other. From the more parochial perspective of the United States, the following issues stand out: the declining dominance of the United States in world economic, social, and political matters; the changing role of government in American life; the question of how to exploit the increasingly rich diversity of our population; and the challenge of renewing our economic capacity. It is imperative that we as a society find an effective set of strategies to maximize our creative potential in this new environment.

For Michigan, the imperative of change is even more striking. The state and its people stand at a critical moment of transition. The question for us is: Can the state of Michigan continue to be a crucible for new ideas, new concepts, and new products that will contribute to the development of a better world for us all? Our history is proud but our future is less certain. Can we, as a region, develop our considerable resources into a new and effective strategy for the future?

We have the resources to play a major economic and social role again. In the international distribution of production we have some natural advantages—particularly in certain types of manufacturing. Michigan's future economic growth will depend on our capacity to assemble an increasingly skilled labor force, modernized plants and equipment, and a menu of new technological developments. In addition, and in the long run more importantly, we have to ensure the existence of appropriate economic, social, and political institutions that will enable us to realize both our cultural and our economic potential.

New knowledge of all kinds will create a new set of possibilities for us, but these can only be actualized if our social institutions—the ways in which we relate to one another—allow us to deploy these resources effectively. Finding a new and effective path to our future development will demand new levels of partnership and commitment. Success will require the dedication of the entire spectrum of our regional institutions and interest groups, management, labor, government, foundations, and universities. Only with such cooperation can we make a reality out of what is now just a possibility.

Paradox, Change, and Choice:
An Economist's View of Some Current
Health Care Resource Issues

While any balanced discussion of our national health sector is inevitably both a celebration and a challenge, the present analysis will focus mainly on a subset of the challenges. My emphasis on the difficulties that lie ahead reflects not a lack of appreciation for the enormous vitality of medicine but a desire to facilitate those changes that will serve society's long-run best interests. In particular, I will focus on what is now known throughout the U.S. health care delivery system as "the cost containment issue." This complex, multidimensional subject involves institutions, individuals, values, economics, ethics, change, science, and, in some respects, life itself.

Although the cost containment issue is usually presented in financial terms—often as new initiatives in health care financing—standing behind those financial issues are much more important and basic changes in the operation of the health care delivery system. What are often advertised as new cost containment strategies are actually strategies aimed at changing the behavior of health care professionals, changing modes of practice, and changing the behavior of patients. They may even stimulate a somewhat different view of the relation between health and the delivery of medical care. In brief, the cost containment issue is simply a politically convenient or polite shorthand for calling into question important components of the current institutional arrangements, values, and perceptions that govern our health care delivery system. Public policies and private initiatives designed to limit the flow of resources into the medical care system signal a widespread desire to alter existing arrangements within this sector or to spend our national wealth on other human needs.

As an economist, I hope I can help clarify some of these issues.

A nation's gross national product (GNP), after all, is only interesting if it reveals something about the performance of the economy in meeting important human needs. Economic analysis can also be helpful when there are insufficient resources to meet all legitimate demands and choices must be made. This is precisely the situation faced by our society in assessing appropriate resource allocations to the health sector and by our medical care delivery system in deciding how best to deploy these resources.

Medicine is not only a science and a profession but an industry that consumes large quantities of human and physical capital and uses these resources to generate impressive quantities of products (e.g., pharmaceuticals), ideas (e.g., new science), trained personnel (e.g., nurses, physicians), and health services (e.g., individual treatments, water purification, and sewage disposal mechanisms). Indeed, in the United States medicine is now a major industry employing more than seven million people. Like any other industry, medicine employs natural resources, facilities, and people (generating costs) to produce products and services (generating value). That is, all industries incur costs and produce socially useful output for which they receive revenues and, one would hope, profits.

If a particular effort (industry) at transforming inputs into outputs is no longer considered sufficiently valuable, it is discontinued. This, for example, has been the fate of the family farm, wooden spokes for wheels, as well as certain types of steel, consumer electronics, and textiles. Similarly, many key decision makers—corporations, government agencies, and labor unions—are now asking whether the institutions and policies governing our medical care delivery are producing the right products and services (allocative efficiency) in the most efficient manner (technical efficiency). That is, they are concerned about whether we are receiving adequate value for the resources we are committing to this sector.

I have emphasized this elementary relation between costs and values to make a second point. Rhetoric regarding costs or cost containment cannot be usefully considered apart from values produced. It is significant that the current debate is framed in terms of cost containment rather than value containment.[1] The debate on health care costs can be further illuminated by a sketch of the historical path by which we arrived at the present juncture.

Some Ancient History: Medicine as Art

From the very beginning of civilization, human beings have dreamed of supplementing the healing forces of nature with direct intervention. Some of the earliest fossil remains of human settlement contain evidence of what might loosely be called neurosurgery. Homer and Herodotus wrote admirably about Egyptian medicine; the Greeks attempted to develop the first rational framework for the study of medicine; pharmacopoeia from the earliest times had residual benefits; Vesalius made advances in anatomy and Harvey in blood circulation in the sixteenth and seventeenth centuries; and there have been prominent physicians and medical investigators in every recorded era. But despite this substantial history, medicine first became scientific in fact rather than intention in the nineteenth century.

It was also during the nineteenth century that the number of hospitals increased dramatically, yet the primary purpose of these institutions was to provide not medical care but free shelter for the sick poor. Hospitals were originally financed by a mixture of philanthropy, donations, public subsidies, and, to a very limited extent, payment from patients. Physicians donated their services; many younger ones actually paid to work there, believing that their practices might benefit from such a service.

By 1900, however, hospitals were finding that the number of their patient days had risen sharply, while the income from their endowments remained relatively constant. The charity basis on which most voluntary hospitals had operated was no longer viable. In 1898 Johns Hopkins decided to enlarge its revenues by increasing charges to its private patients and charging them for physicians' services. Other hospitals soon followed. Further, as medical knowledge burgeoned, patient payments again had to be raised to meet rising costs. Physicians began to charge hospital patients for their services, thereby altering forever the relationship between doctor and patient.

Contemporary Medicine as Science and Industry

Contemporary medicine stands completely transformed from its ancient but rather humble history. Only in this century has medicine become a respected scientific profession, capable of both individual and large-scale interventions that effectively alter the course of various diseases and engineer stunning changes in the world's epidemiological map. Despite variations in the contemporary health delivery systems of industrialized societies, they all participate in an unprecedented and striking alteration of medicine from art to science and from an activity of minor significance to an industry with considerable social, political, and economic impact. Perhaps the most concrete and visible sign of this change is the revolutionary transformation of hospitals from "warehouses of human misery" where no one would choose to go, let alone pay for the privilege, to institutions uniquely capable of complex and highly valued medical/surgical interventions.

It is, therefore, appropriate to consider the twentieth century as a revolutionary period in the history of medicine. I emphasize these radical changes because the health care delivery system is undergoing a dynamic evolution. It is not a mature system from which only slow, marginal alterations are to be expected. On the contrary, it is a young, quickly evolving system from which we can continue to expect extraordinary transmutations.

Although the U.S. health care delivery system has changed continuously throughout most of this century, the last two decades have been unusually eventful. Since 1965 the U.S. medical service industry has undergone a major metamorphosis, with one achievement topping another. Why, then, at precisely this moment in our history, are we worried about containing health care costs and restructuring certain aspects of medical care delivery? An analysis of this apparent paradox requires some celebration.

After all, progress in medical science has been spectacular. The news media report almost daily advances in medical science, followed closely by application of this new knowledge to clinical situations. Our capacity to understand, intervene in, and alter the course of various diseases has grown beyond all but the most fertile imaginations of a generation ago.

There have been other types of advances as well. In 1965 the notion of equal access to health care, an essential component of equal opportunity, was largely hollow rhetoric. Yet the gap between rich and poor has substantially narrowed in the last two decades, as indicated by current demographic data on participation in serious kinds of surgery as well as on the use of hospitals and other important medical services. Obviously, some segments of our population are still underserved. Many of our private and public medical assistance programs are in trouble, and many hospitals, particularly inner-city teaching hospitals, still face significant problems in uncompensated care. Nevertheless, enormous progress has been made in this area. Clearly, the medically indigent have been far better served by broad-scale government action—such as Medicare, Medicaid, Hill-Burton, medical education—and broad-based health insurance initiatives than they were by the dispensary and donated physician services in times past.

These and other developments have led to significant decreases in mortality rates from such major conditions as heart disease and stroke. Medical education has expanded both here and abroad, yielding a 75 percent growth in the number of physicians and even larger increases in the numbers of other health care workers. Wages of physicians have been at least adequate (usually more than adequate) since the beginning of this century, but in the last twenty years the wages of other hospital workers have significantly improved. People no longer have to have a "calling" to work in hospitals.

Two other important developments, however, accompanied these achievements. First, a major new force entered the medical industry: the third party payer, principally the federal government and private health insurance companies. In 1965 direct payments by individuals accounted for just under 50 percent of all expenditures for medical care and private insurance for an additional 18 percent. The federal government's share stood at about 12 percent—approximately equal to that of state and local governments. Two decades later direct payments by individuals have shrunk to just over 25 percent, the private insurance share has almost doubled to over 25 percent, and the federal government's portion has more than doubled to over 30 percent. Medicare and Medicaid patients are popularly thought to account for virtually all of this substantial increase in the federal government's support of medical services. But because health care has been a tax-free benefit, families earning over $32,000 per year consume well over one-fourth of the federal resource contribution to medical care.

Second, health expenditures began to account for over 10 percent of the nation's GNP, compared with just 6 percent two decades ago. Furthermore, since the GNP increased substantially in this period, health care was consuming a larger slice of a significantly larger pie. These enormous advances, then, were bought at a considerable cost. In the last two decades health expenditures per capita have grown from $211 to $1,300, or at an average annual rate of 12.5 percent. This is twice the growth rate of the economy as a whole. In addition, new public policies and health financing arrangements have caused federal budgets to skyrocket. Federal expenditures for health have increased 300 percent *after* adjustment for inflation and before the substantial aging of our population—a figure that would rivet any congressperson's attention.

These statistics are important because the changes we anticipate in the health care sector will result not primarily from advances in the profession or science of medicine but from the budgetary actions of the federal government. These actions are motivated by overall fiscal concerns, perceived threats to resources available for other desirable programs, and a sociopolitical balancing of society's needs and resources. Thus the issues are politically loaded.

The health care sector has not only consumed more resources but has also encountered an unusually rapid escalation of prices. Since 1960 the consumer price index has about tripled. During the same period, however, the price of hospital services has risen tenfold. Physician fees are between 4 and 5 times what they were and the price of other forms of medical care about 3.5 times. Further, this superinflationary tendency has accelerated since 1978, with health care costs rising faster than taxes, energy costs, or the wages of labor union members. At a time when inflation has captured the attention of most Americans, the soaring price of health services has naturally drawn concern.

The impetus to curb these costs emanates from a number of sources. Pressure on the federal budget has led to the development of diagnosis related groups (DRGs) and other initiatives. State governments, responding to similar pressure, have begun to treat the medically indigent less generously. Other changes arise from the operation of more-or-less private markets. The greater supply of physicians, a very slowly growing population, the adoption of prepaid plans, new competition among private health insurers, and economies of scale have also caused competitive pressures that threaten the livelihood of some physicians and hospitals. These market forces reflect the same basic aims as those underlying the budget actions of federal and state government, namely, the more efficient and appropriate use of resources in the health care sector.

New Politics and New Questions

As these various forces in the health care sector have continued to evolve, public attitudes have undergone a significant transformation. Only two decades ago Lyndon Johnson articulated the following theme for America during his presidential campaign: "The federal government can do a lot of things for the people and we are going to do them all!" The Great Society program he subsequently implemented included not only Medicare and Medicaid, but also new initiatives with neighborhood health centers, community mental health centers, the health service corps, and improved funding for medical education and research. New financial incentives—including fee-for-service, first dollar coverage, and cost-based reimbursement—were designed to expand both the quality and availability of health care services.

How different these initiatives sound from today's watchwords: copayments, deductibles, DRGs, frozen fee schedules, and Medicare vouchers. After two decades of cheering for the rapid advances in the health care profession, we have begun listening to the growing chorus of concern for the strain these advances have put on our national resources. The question posed by the health policies of the Great Society—how can we maximize both the quantity and quality of medical care delivered?—has been replaced by a set of questions regarding efficiencies, the appropriate emphasis on acute care, the role of technology, health financing practices, and the actual relation between medical care and health. These new questions probe many of the existing arrangements and policies by which we deliver medical care. Let us consider some of them more carefully.

First, take the question of efficiency, that is, of whether the medical sector is using resources as effectively as possible. What, for example, are the implications of the standard cost-based payment mechanisms for hospital efficiency? From an economist's point of view, a cost-based payment mechanism can be expected to lead to overcapitalization, inefficiency, and excess capacity. In fact, this is exactly what happened in the hospital industry. Resources were inefficiently deployed, and wages of hospital workers were higher than those for similar occupations in other industries. Designers of the Great Society programs, who understood though perhaps underestimated these forces, chose to rely on regulations to counterbalance the incentives for overexpansion and inefficiency because their overriding concern was expansion of and access to quality health services.[2] Obviously, regulation has failed to ensure adequate efficiency in the use of the nation's resources. Moreover, while cost-based financing may address issues of access and quality, it also encouraged complex procedures at marginally qualified institutions, leading to higher-than-necessary mortality rates.

What about the efficiency implications of fee-for-service? In this system the purely economic incentives lead only to inefficiency: maximizing expenditures and service delivery whether needed or not, ignoring cost-benefit considerations, and paying for care rendered rather than benefit received. Other questions arise with respect to the professional organization of physicians and professional fees. Why, for instance, have professional fees not been significantly reduced for procedures that were initially difficult, risky, and infrequent but are now low-risk and routine, such as coronary bypass surgery, cardiac catheterization, and gastrointestinal endoscopy?

Any payment mechanism—whether fee-for-service, fee-per-diagnosis, or capitation scheme—incorporates a particular set of economic incentives that will affect the behavior of both patient and provider. Thus the optimal mechanism will change as our objectives change. From the economic perspective the payment mechanism of the last two decades offered no reward to the consumer for seeking out an efficient provider and no motivation for the provider to become efficient. Our overall societal goals remain accessibility, quality, and efficiency, but we are rethinking the appropriate social definition of quality, the relative importance of efficiency, and our willingness to keep committing resources to existing institutions and practices.

There are also new questions about the relation between medical care and health. We know that medical care can often be essential for health, but in many cases it has only a modest effect. And although the medical care sector consumes most of the resources devoted to health care, many observers now believe that behavior is the chief determinant of health. With mounting evidence that environment and life-style crucially affect health, we are beginning to realize, first, that the resources expended on the medical care sector do not always directly correlate with actual health outcomes and, second, that resources spent outside the existing health care delivery system may have a greater impact.

We are also asking other questions, first posed by Victor Fuchs, such as why the medical care industry consists of so many seemingly artificial separations. Why, for instance, do we separate inpatient from outpatient care, personal from public health issues, health services from social services? What we know about human development makes it clear that these issues are intimately related. Do we deliver overly elaborate care to some, and too much care in an inpatient setting? On the consumer side, we are questioning what impact prepayment and "first dollar coverage" have on consumer demand since these practices provide little incentive for the prudent use of health services.

We are asking that the role of medical technology be reassessed in order to identify and perhaps eliminate marginally useful, unnecessary, and redundant practices and procedures. Although the correlation may be spurious, rapidly escalating medical costs (values?) have been associated—even by those in the medical profession—with the introduction of much new medical technology. Some observers believe that this technology, which accounts for many of the most significant advances in contemporary medicine, merely substitutes one nuisance for another at greatly increased costs rather than enabling a new quality of care. At the very least we seem to be faced with the dilemma of either introducing fewer advances from clinical research into patient care or continuing to devote larger and larger portions of our GNP to medical care. Technology in other sectors, however, is associated with decreasing costs or the capacity to meet certain needs with fewer resources. In part the apparent anomaly of medical technology can be attributed to semantic problems and incomplete accounting. That is, we count the costs of a new nuclear magnetic resonance (NMR) facility but not the benefits to patients of the improved technology. If the medical sector wishes to attract adequate resources for the continued development and introduction of new technologies—many of which may reduce costs—we must devise a better framework for discussing this issue.

In addition to and underlying all these factors, however, we are asking whether the entire institutional structure that has evolved for medical care in this country continues to serve our long-run best interest and the best interest of our citizens' health. Given current national resource commitments, this is an entirely appropriate question. We must continue to evaluate the existing health care structure with an eye to the more efficient use of those resources that society devotes to medical care. The "cost containment issue" is simply the title of the national drama that concerns how we may best organize medical care delivery for the next decades.

Fundamental to the current status of health care delivery are three conditions that interest economists. First, the delivery of health care consumes real resources: people, capital equipment, buildings, and time. Second, these individual and national resources are scarce in relation to human needs; that is, we do not have enough people, equipment, or raw material to meet all human needs. Thus whenever we commit resources to the medical care sector, we are preventing them from flowing to other human needs. Third, individuals adhere to varying values and preferences: not everyone ranks medical care as their first priority. In such situations economists like to ask how we allocate resources to alternative uses when individual desires and values vary greatly.

These conditions contrast sharply with the Great Society premise that our resources were somehow unlimited or else that our values would lead us voluntarily to allocate as many of our resources as necessary to the health care sector. Today, as contemporary public policy discussions attest, we are no longer willing unquestioningly to assign as many of our resources as the medical sector deems necessary to fulfill its function. Instead we are asking for some accounting of costs and benefits.

To ensure an adequate flow of national resources to medical care, we will have to change our institutions, practices, and behavior. In particular, we will have to make many traditional practices and attitudes more efficient. We must, for example, break down the barriers between personal and public health, between inpatient and outpatient health services and social services. We may have to reconsider the relation between physicians and patients, between physicians and other health professionals (such as nurses), among physicians themselves, and among physicians, patients, and hospitals. By remaining attached to the status quo, the health care sector will, in my opinion, only attenuate the level of resources that society is willing to devote to medical care.

With its current belief in a limited national capacity, society will demand that health care providers become accountable for the efficient use of resources. The public will insist on greater variety in the mode of health care delivery and on clarification of the relation between resources used in the medical care sector and the resulting health of the population. We may even need to evolve a new understanding of what is meant by health and quality care. Vital ethical as well as economic and medical issues are involved. In short, we not only want to look at cost/benefit ratios, but also to clarify what is meant by benefits.

At the same time, we must guard against too narrow an outlook. Medical care costs are the product of two elements: the quantity of care delivered and the price per unit of that care. One way to constrain medical care costs is to decrease the quantity or quality of care delivered. That may be happening right now, and the prospect of further rationing medical care is clearly before us. Critical aspects of the DRG system, for example, yield few incentives for quality care or the most complex acute care services, and many other efficiency measures (e.g., fewer tests, shorter hospital stays) may also lower quality. Further, to the extent that Medicare/Medicaid programs offer less advantageous terms for their clients, providers may decide not to offer their services to this segment of the population. Indeed it could be argued that the DRG system will result in allocating a greater share of medical services to the best served part of the population—the higher income group. It would be disappointing to return to a two-tier system of health care.

Underlying the issues of cost containment, DRGs, and other payment mechanisms are the questions of what health means and how we can more efficiently and appropriately use our national resources. Not only do we wish to use our resources as efficiently as possible in support of particular activities, but we want to ensure that the most effective set of activities (e.g., acute care versus preventive care versus environmental issues) is pursued.

Contemporary cost containment issues, such as DRGs, are only the first step in our ongoing reevaluation of health and health care delivery. By setting up new financial incentives aimed at alter-

ing the behavior of those in the medical care industry, our government and society at large are asking for efficiency and limitation of
service rather than expansion of service and revenue. This is far from
the last word on the subject. Unacceptable aspects of this initial
system will undoubtedly be revised.

At the moment, however, the federal government is focusing
on the hospital as the site of change, hoping that this new set of
incentives will force hospitals to assume the responsibility for altering the behavior of patients, physicians, and other health care professionals. Hospitals have, I think, been singled out for two basic reasons. First, the Medicare/Medicaid budget is one of the principal
driving elements in this particular reform, and most Medicare/
Medicaid payments go to hospitals or related activities. Second,
these financial incentives mask some difficult political and social
decisions. Under this new mechanism hospitals will have to decide
what services to offer, to whom to offer them, how many indigent
patients to take, which diseases to treat, and what procedures and
practices are financially viable. It is much easier for Congress to
legislate economic incentives than to confront the political and social realities of decisions regarding health care expenditures. Thus,
many health care providers will face these sensitive social, medical,
and ethical issues on their own. Something as deceptively simple as
DRGs has placed an enormous burden on their shoulders.

Policy makers will, I believe, continue to focus on the groups
and institutions providing health care and to encourage fuller coordi-
nation among health management practices such as inpatient and
outpatient services, medical and social services. For the health care
sector this implies both *change* and *choice*. With respect to *change*,
standard practices and procedures must be reevaluated. We may
have to alter how we think about health care and how medical care
delivery relates to ultimate health outcomes. Perhaps, for appropriate or inappropriate reasons, we will develop new standards and
definitions of quality care.

Medical education may also have to change. It is no longer
clear, for example, that we can afford the rapidly rising faculty/
student ratios in medical schools or support the existing number of
residencies in various specialty programs. We do not know who will
pay for graduate medical education or clinical research, and current
federal initiatives do not solve this problem. Finally, the viability of

our teaching hospitals must be examined: it is not clear how they will evolve and whether they will remain the centers of advanced tertiary care they are today. In the last decade the academic health center has become a focal point of education, research, and patient care, and these elements have become so intimately intertwined that they will be difficult to separate. But changes are certain to come; all physicians, nurses, administrators, and allied health professionals will have to change much of what they do and how they think about their work.

With respect to *choice,* society is unwilling to allocate enough resources to meet all the legitimate aspirations of U.S. health care providers, so difficult choices will have to be made. If my interpretation of our social history is correct, the American people will turn first to the medical profession for advice on what choices should be made. That profession, therefore, has both the opportunity and the obligation for leadership. But society has not waited and will not wait. If the medical profession does not offer creative ideas, someone else—less informed and perhaps less able—will.

Exerting leadership means accepting the tension that will inevitably accompany change—tension, for instance, in the traditional physician-patient and physician-physician relations. It also means reexamining the premises underlying much of the profession's behavior for the last two decades—for instance, the resource-intensive demands of specialist training programs. Previous behavior was appropriate, even exemplary, for its time, but new times demand new ideas. In particular, leadership requires looking beyond the purely parochial interest of medical care providers. Only by broadening our vision can we expect others, such as the government, to listen to our concerns.

The future viability of the U.S. health sector depends, in great measure, on the leadership of the medical profession. In the decades ahead, leadership will require not only professional skill but flexibility, tolerance for ambiguity and uncertainty, and the capacity to identify and implement new modes of practice and treatment. Most of all, these actions must exhibit a breadth of vision and commitment that comprehends not only developments in medical science but also our society's broadest set of needs and resources. I hope the present essay will move us in this direction.

The helpful comments of my colleagues Professors Paul J. Feldstein, S. Martin Lindenauer, and George D. Zuidema are noted.

1. The national debate on cost containment suffers a second material deficiency by failing to acknowledge that unless we understand which components of cost we are trying to contain (quantity of care, quality of care, prices of medical services, and so on), the rhetoric is not very helpful. A prerequisite of an informed debate is to look behind aggregate costs at their individual components, upon which public policy and market forces could exert real behavioral impact. The details really matter.

2. Contrary to myth, the U.S. health delivery system has relied on government regulation through most of this century. Importantly, the government has regulated various public health issues, including drugs, and has delegated most other issues to the medical profession.

The Federal Role in U.S. Higher Education

The legitimate object of government is to do for a community
of people whatever they need to have done, but cannot do at
all in their separate and individual capacities.
                                                  —Abraham Lincoln

Despite the limitations imposed by an inhospitable constitutional framework, the U.S. government has always played a part in higher education and, in more recent decades, that involvement has steadily grown. This essay argues for an enhanced federal role in the financing of higher education. Rather than developing a complete rationale to support my view, I will consider only certain core arguments and their implications for the last decades of the twentieth century.

In the first place, formal education in the United States—as distinct from on-the-job training—represents a major national resource commitment, consuming approximately 7 percent of the gross national product. In the 1980–81 academic year this commitment totaled just under $200 billion, or approximately $3,500 per enrolled student; higher education accounted for about a third of this amount (just over $70 billion, or 2.5 percent of the GNP)—an average expenditure of $4,525 per full-time equivalent student.

In 1929, by contrast, the U.S. commitment to higher education absorbed less than 1 percent of the GNP. Adjusted for inflation, this means that over the last five decades support per student has risen by about 1.4 percent a year, or 68 percent altogether. These overall averages, however, mask an actual drop in the constant dollar investment per full-time equivalent student in the 1930s, 1940s, and 1970s. Only in the 1950s and 1960s did support per student really grow.

The federal government's contribution to this enterprise is currently about $17 billion, or 2.5 percent of its budget, which amounts to between 15 and 20 percent of higher education's current revenues. The most important components of this assistance are the various forms of student financial aid (over 50 percent of the federal commitment—$9 billion in 1980) and support of particular research programs (over 20 percent—$3.5 billion in 1980). About 17 percent of this commitment comes indirectly through certain tax benefits, including tax exemptions claimable by parents of full-time students, exclusions of many scholarships and fellowships from taxable income, and favorable tax treatment of contributions to higher education. A final type of assistance—direct support for institutions through grants of land or money or special programs for buildings or equipment—has always been modest. Through these substantial contributions the government significantly influences certain sectors of American higher education.

Despite this commitment of federal resources, direct responsibility for education—including higher education—remains vested either in the individual states or in various private organizations. Among industrialized nations, only the United States and Canada politically decentralize the responsibility for higher education, and only the United States economically decentralizes it as well. Both Canada and the United States are, of course, political federations that maintain a delicate balance of federal and local responsibilities. Despite an initial commitment to regional responsibilities for higher education, virtually all other contemporary political federations (e.g., Switzerland, Australia, West Germany) have come to believe that present-day higher education requires a major federal role. For the majority of developed countries, modern universities are indispensable to realizing national priorities, and the governments of most such countries will not allow narrowly defined constitutional issues or outdated traditions to frustrate important national objectives.

The U.S. government, however, has never articulated a comprehensive or purposeful policy with respect to higher education. Perhaps a more comprehensive policy would ill suit our constitutional base and would make it difficult to mediate between federal and state priorities. Whatever the ambiguities of the constitutional provisions governing education, I believe they will permit a fuller division of responsibility for higher education between federal and state government, should such an arrangement serve the national interest. As a prelude to more informed speculation about an appropriate federal role for the future, let us survey the evolution of current attitudes and policies with respect to federal involvement in higher education.

Antecedents

The relationship of higher education to the principal governing institutions of a society tends to reflect the developing technological or social framework of the society as a whole. In medieval Europe the changing relationship of the university to society's central institutions—the Church and the state—clearly mirrored the gradual expansion of the state's sovereignty over that of the Church. Since the university has always been embedded in rather than separate from society, its strength and autonomy had ultimately to derive from other social institutions—in those early years, from either the secular authority of the prince or the sacred authority of the Church.

European higher education began as an integral part of ecclesiastical instruction. But as early as the ninth century, it no longer organized itself completely within the Church hierarchy. By the thirteenth century universities were viewed as separate and distinct bodies, not subservient to Church or state but independent, quasi-legal entities, as the term *universitas* (a society, a community) suggests. This independence was never complete or long-lived, but it remains a cherished tradition in academic life.

The Protestant Reformation greatly accelerated the shift from ecclesiastical to civil law, so that, increasingly, the state, not the Church, ceded privileges to corporations such as the university. The spread of civil law in France, for instance, transformed the university from an independent group of scholars into an agency of the state. In England, too, the state played an ever larger role in universities until, in the mid-nineteenth century, higher education came under considerable parliamentary control. Only the great British universities, Oxford and Cambridge, still symbolize the medieval ideal of the autonomous community.

In Germany, governments actually founded and thus strongly regulated universities from the beginning. Not until the nineteenth century did Alexander von Humboldt incorporate the ideal of independence and academic freedom into the University of Berlin. Thus, European universities emerged in their present form, in part, as a product of the conflict between Church and state, with the state even today exercising significant, if not dominant, control over them. What autonomy exists in European universities—and it is often considerable—is viewed as a privilege, not a right.

The American Case

Seen against this backdrop, the American university seems anomalous. Majority congressional opinion has always considered all education to be a responsibility of state and local governments, private individuals, and corporations. That notable experiment, Harvard College, was established in 1636 by the colony of Massachusetts, not—as it should have been under British law—by the Crown. Interestingly, despite its status as a "private" institution, Harvard received regular grants from the colony (later the Commonwealth) of Massachusetts. The distinction between public and private institutions has always been blurry because both receive various direct and indirect government subsidies. More important to the history of the private university in the United States was the Supreme Court decision in the famous Dartmouth College case (1819): to the question of whether all institutions incorporated under government charter were publicly controlled, the justices answered a resounding "no."

Private colleges flourished alongside state-sponsored colleges and universities. By 1950 each accounted for about the same number of students, although there were almost six times as many private as public institutions. In the following three decades, enrollment in higher education more than doubled at private institutions but rose by over 500 percent at the nation's public universities. By 1980 public institutions claimed 78 percent of all enrollments and approximately two-thirds of all expenditures.

The recent concern about the appropriate federal role in higher education actually continues a debate on that subject begun in colonial times. The idea of establishing a national university was advanced by such diverse individuals as George Washington, Thomas Jefferson, and John Quincy Adams. As a matter of national policy, Congress decided not to adopt such plans but to place the primary obligation for public higher education on the states. Nevertheless, in 1787—the same year the Constitution was ratified—Congress passed the Northwest Ordinance, which established land grants for educational institutions in the new U.S. territories. Thus began a century and a half of what could be described as a steady trickle of federal support for higher education.

In 1802 the U.S. Military Academy was founded, and by 1830 the first federal research contract had been granted to the Franklin Institute. In 1879 Howard University became one of the few institutions other than the service academies to be chartered by the federal government.

The first Morrill Act (1862) built on the Northwest Ordinance, setting aside additional public lands for land-grant colleges, which were to be chartered by the states. The language of the act cloaked the federal government's part in higher education in politically acceptable rhetoric: "the orderly disposition of public lands," "the betterment of agriculture," and "the promotion of the arts." Colleges were enjoined to teach agriculture and the mechanical and military arts without neglecting the classical curriculum. The federal dollars involved were designated as a permanent endowment of the colleges established under the act; states were not permitted to divert them to building and maintenance expenses. As a federal initiative, the land-grant universities in general exemplify the profound influence of the U.S. government on the shape of higher education in this country. With their rapid expansion of curriculum and their availability to a much wider, more diverse student body, these institutions marked a radical transformation in American higher education.

The Hatch Act (1887) established a series of stations for agricultural experiments and, in a new departure for a federal initiative, authorized direct annual payments to educational institutions, thus bypassing the states entirely. The second Morrill Act of 1890 allocated to the land-grant institutions funds for instruction in agriculture and industry and, later, for training education and health professionals. This act had several notable features. It doubled the federal contribution to land-grant colleges, but it also specified procedures that have controlled federal aid to higher education ever since—determining what subjects of inquiry would receive government support, requiring detailed annual reports, and instituting penalties for noncompliance with federal regulations.

During the following decades a series of acts provided modest support for agriculture, home economics, and vocational education, as well as, in 1916, setting up the Reserve Officers' Training Corps on college and university campuses. In 1937, the National Cancer Institute was established, and the first fellowships for public health service were offered. During the 1930s other forms of financial aid legislation were enacted as well. In the years following World War II, however, the unsteady and unpredictable trickle of federal resources committed to higher education deepened into a river, with at least some sense of direction.

In 1944 the Servicemen's Readjustment Act (the GI Bill) provided federal support for veterans wishing to pursue higher education. By 1948, one-half of all male college students had federal support of some kind. The 1958 National Defense Education Act accelerated the training of students in science and math in an effort to "catch up" with the Russians after the launching of Sputnik. Bemused by this piece of legislation, Robert M. Hutchins noted that

> History will smile sardonically at the spectacle of this great country getting interested slightly and temporarily in education only because of the technical advancements of Russia, and then being able to act as a nation only by assimilating education into a cold war and calling an education bill a defense act.

Yet Hutchins's analysis was not entirely correct. Individual states had already made substantial investments, and the federal government had funded some piecemeal initiatives in higher education over the previous century. Moreover, a minority in Congress had always supported a larger federal role in higher education. Perhaps Hutchins's point was that the federal government always subsumed its concern for colleges and universities under some other purpose, such as the Cold War.

In the post–World War II period, the U.S. government also undertook the funding of university-based research. In 1945 the Fulbright Act began financing the international exchange of scholars. Later the National Science Foundation (1950) and the National Foundations for the Arts and for the Humanities (1965) were established to supply research funding for individual scholars, programs, and institutions. These actions helped make research one of the leading missions of American universities and made American universities the major vehicle of the nation's efforts in basic research. Thus, another set of federal initiatives once again transformed the nature of American higher education.

President Johnson's Great Society program added another crucial dimension to federal support of higher education. The Johnson Administration's goal of ending poverty and inequality led to a series of important student financial aid initiatives. Access to higher education was broadened by means of the College Work-Study Program and the National Direct Student Loan Program, both enacted in 1965. The Higher Education Act, also passed in 1965, included the Guaranteed Student Loan program and the Educational Opportunity Grant (EOG) program. In 1972 the EOG program became the Basic Educational Opportunity Grants—now called Pell Grants—and the Supplemental Educational Opportunity Grants, considerably expanding funding sources for students. The Middle Income Student Assistance Act of 1978 extended Basic Grants to families with higher incomes, setting out formulas to determine their appropriate level of support. Over the last decades, then, despite what many consider a shaky constitutional footing, the federal presence in higher education—under one banner or another—has steadily gained ground.

Toward a Reconsideration of the Federal Role in Higher Education

With this history as background, I contend that the federal government should assume a greater role in higher education because of its responsibilities in two areas: national economic development and equal opportunity. Other characteristics of higher education, of course, also directly concern the federal government, but the present discussion will focus on only these two.

With respect to economic development, many maintain that improved training and research are essential ingredients of technological progress and economic growth. And indeed, so much of America's best research talent is located in universities that any decline in federal support would substantially weaken our national efforts in science and technology. But it is not only scientific developments that determine the creation and spread of new technology. As I have argued elsewhere, there are three key determinants of economic growth: (1) the educational attainment and health of the work force and its capacity for adaptation and change; (2) capital growth, that is, the installation of new plants and equipment; and (3) technological advances and their adaptation. Because of its responsibility for the welfare of the national economy, the federal government must strive to secure an adequate aggregate investment in all three of these principal sources of our economic growth.

Ironically, it is widely agreed that there must be federal support (e.g., through tax credits) for investment in nonhuman capital such as machines and buildings, but there is no corresponding consensus about the federal responsibility for investment in human capital. In the future, the key to successful competition in the international economic arena will be the training and adaptability of our labor force, that is, the quality of our human capital. Technical skills and understanding will be a necessary, but not a sufficient, characteristic of such a labor force. Even more important will be the ability to analyze and solve new problems and the capacity to form and re-form new social, political, and economic institutions that will allow us to maximize our society's creative potential. More than ever before, then, it is critical that the federal government guarantee our national investment in human capital through training and education—especially liberal education.

Given the mobility of capital and labor in our national economy, moreover, the federal government has more incentives than the individual states to secure optimal investment in human capital, physical capital, and science. Why should the state of North Dakota, for example, invest $15,000 or $20,000 a year in a medical student who may choose to practice in South Dakota or Florida? The same argument holds in the area of scientific research, whose benefits cannot be confined by state boundaries. Various levels of government, as well as private individuals and groups, share in the advantages of higher education and should therefore all share in its costs.

A second reason for an expanded federal role in higher education is one that has long been at the heart of our national social policy: equal opportunity. If access to higher education is restricted to those who can afford it, both the universities and our society will be diminished. The talents and abilities of all our citizens will need to be fully realized if we are to solve the full array of problems currently before us. As in the past, the federal government has a shared but direct responsibility for maintaining equal access to educational opportunity.

Throughout our history, federal initiatives in higher education have responded only to specific challenges and addressed only particular problems. To be most effective, support for higher education must promote the national interest without undermining the strength of our pluralistic approach to education. In the particular climate of the late twentieth century, such considerations suggest the need for a more systematic and fully articulated federal role in funding higher education.

I conclude with three cautions. First, we must carefully design our vehicles for federal support in ways that foster underlying national objectives such as the pursuit of excellence or the promotion of equal opportunity. Second, as they work to establish a fuller partnership with the federal government in financing higher education, states and private organizations should be careful not to mistake the federal interest as equal to their own. That is, we must safeguard the benefits of our pluralism. Finally, we in higher education must demonstrate our worthiness for such increased attention. It is not ordained that college presidents, college faculties, and college students be richly endowed. We must earn our share of the nation's resources by showing that we are shaping a better world.

The Organization
and Management of
the University

Critic and Servant: The Role of the University

Inaugural Address, April 14, 1980

It is an honor for me to be able to serve the University of Michigan as its tenth president. As a university of international distinction, Michigan today can proudly point to thriving programs in teaching and scholarship in the sciences, in the social sciences, in the humanities, in the creative and performing arts, and in the professions. Such a wide spectrum of efforts is typical of public universities in America, but the overall quality and excellence of Michigan's current programs places its among the relatively few truly distinguished universities, public or private, in this country. Moreover, the university can bear witness to a long tradition of such distinction in education and scholarship.

This achievement is the result of an enduring and unique collaboration between the university's faculty, its students, its alumni and friends, and the citizens of the state of Michigan. The university today is the historical culmination of the ideas, efforts, and resources of this dynamic partnership, and the partners have every reason to be proud of the result. Their efforts and vision have realized a very special idea, the idea of distinction in a large public university. This idea was given substance by the continuing commitment of the university community and its supporters to participate in an exciting and exacting intellectual voyage whose destination lay at the forefront of scholarship, teaching, and research.

The journey has not always been untroubled or placid. Rather, an important tradition of general uneasiness and honest skepticism about our own efforts has helped us recognize our shortcomings, adapt to changing times, and thus actively retain our position in the world of scholarship. In the coming decades, we will be challenged to find new ways to sustain the university materially and intellectually, but our strong traditions will help teach us what is appropriate and where our priorities should lie.

Of course, the University of Michigan has its origins not only in its own particular conception, but in the more general traditions of higher education in America. I would like to consider certain aspects of this more general tradition in order to sharpen our perception of the relationship between the university and society and its future prospects.

American universities have their roots in the universities of medieval Europe. Even the ivy was brought from the university in Salerno to the walls of many of our earliest universities. A very important additional infusion of European influences came from the German universities of the nineteenth century, where modern training in science was being pioneered. In the United States, however, these influences underwent many important transformations in the construction of our distinctive system of higher education.

One of the more significant transformations, in my judgment, was that American universities were always responsible to and, to a certain extent, shaped by the communities that founded them. Unlike certain of their European counterparts, they were never completely self-governing bodies of scholars and students.

Thus, from the very beginning, American universities had to balance their responsibilities to the world of scholarship with important responsibilities to the communities that supported them. This was true of the early private universities as well as the great public universities that followed them. This tradition has important consequences for the current role of American universities and their responsibilities in our society.

The relationship between the modern university and society is very complex and fragile because of the university's dual role as society's servant and as society's critic. On the one hand, the university has the responsibility for training and research functions that serve society's current economic and cultural life. On the other hand, the university has a fundamental responsibility to criticize society's current arrangements and to construct, entertain, and test alternative ways of organizing society's institutions, alternative approaches to understanding nature, and alternative visions of society's values.

Over time, society's support for this dual concept of the university as an institution both serving and criticizing society has been ultimately sustained by faith in rationalism, faith in knowledge and science, and the resulting notion of human progress. Perhaps one of the most distinctive ideas of Western civilization is the idea that nature, by itself, cannot achieve its full potential. Rather, what is needed is a mutually beneficial interaction among nature, science, and humankind. The university plays an increasingly central role in this process. In the end, we all live under the sway of ideas, and the idea of progress in both our material and our moral or spiritual condition has increasingly dominated Western thought. In my view, the university now plays a critical role in strengthening the positive correlation between progress in science and the development of new knowledge, and progress in the moral and spiritual sense.

As we look to the future of our universities and their relationship to society, however, it is important to look specifically at the nature of our educational and research programs. Are these programs adequate to support the traditional dual roles of the university as society's servant and society's critic?

What are the specific types of programmatic objectives that enable the universities to meet their responsibilities to the world of scholarship and to the society of which they are a part? We can, I believe, identify three major categories of necessary commitments in this respect.

1. The responsibility for general and professional education
2. The responsibility for the development of new knowledge
3. The responsibility for advanced research training

To amplify my view of the university's responsibility for general and professional education, let me suggest that the ultimate purpose of a general education is twofold. The first goal is to provide students with an understanding of what our society is, how it came to be that way, and how it relates to the larger human community. The second is to provide our students with the kind of knowledge and understanding that improves their concept of civilization by demonstrating that the concrete present is but one alternative. In this context it is clear that not only training in science, but scholarly exposure to history, literature, and philosophy have direct relevance to society's most important goals: this knowledge puts our immediate concerns in the broadest possible human context. Without the understanding that flows from study in the humanities, we must fail to fathom critical dimensions of the human experience and too easily deny the intractability of certain aspects of the human condition. Thus we are responsible for providing an education that not only develops students' technical expertise, but relates their experience to the broad human landscape of which we are a part, moving them to a purpose and capacity beyond themselves.

The same approach governs professional education at a university. Professional education normally refers to the acquisition of skills for a particular purpose. At a university, however, it must also be involved in the extension of knowledge. Further, it must proceed within a critical framework that not only refuses to accept things as they are, but works to bridge the gap between professional practice and theoretical knowledge.

These are the fundamental characteristics of our educational programs that we must preserve in the years ahead. In addition, for reasons I will discuss shortly, our nation has a great stake in maintaining the research capacities of our universities, especially our major research universities. Given our society's needs, attitudes, and resources, what are the prospects for achieving these objectives?

On the one hand, the American public generally perceives our universities to be at some risk in this decade because of expected declines in student enrollments and in available resources. Such developments would, of course, affect not only the educational function and fiscal capacity of universities, but the essential research capacity of our society.

On the other hand, the need for advanced training and research has never been greater. Globally we are on the brink, I believe, of another technological breakthrough in industrial and agricultural processes, and the extent of U.S. participation in these developments and the economic growth that will result is uncertain. Fortunately, or unfortunately, this depends in part on the viability of the major research universities—with which this state is well endowed. In the United States no other institution can fully substitute for the traditional role of the universities in basic research and development. Perhaps by the year 2000 we will have a larger spectrum of research institutions in this country than exists elsewhere. But for the next decades the research and development capacity of the United States is inextricably tied to the health of the research universities.

In addition, we need new, creative ways to deal more effectively with a large number of outstanding social issues. Consider the challenge of the revitalization of the inner cities, the challenge of gaining a full share of society's opportunities for minorities and women, or the challenge of creatively mediating the conflicts that arise from time to time between traditional values and new developments in science. The solutions to these problems—and similar challenges—require careful, critical analysis of alternative ways of doing things and of organizing society's institutions. The need for an informed and thoughtful electorate has never been greater.

Moreover, we can fully anticipate that in the next decades changes in our modes of thinking will be both necessary and substantial. The world will never again be so centered on Western Europe and North America—on the particular cultural history, experiences, and civilization that have dominated world affairs in the last few centuries. We must, therefore, develop a new awareness, openness, and responsibility not only to certain populations in our own society, but to others around the world whose cultural achievement and expression we have yet to appreciate adequately.

For these reasons, and others, I believe our future as a society is importantly related to the vitality of our universities. What other institution can provide the humanistic understanding, the scientific developments, the technical training, the critical analysis, and the aesthetic experiences that can—at their best—produce both the necessary new knowledge and a thoughtful, informed citizenry capable of more wisely meeting the complex challenges of the next decades? The major question that remains, however, is whether and how the society on the one hand and the universities and their faculties on the other will act in order to meet these needs and thus jointly realize our creative potential. Each decade in our history has its own challenges and requires new responses in order to enhance and contribute to what is a noble tradition.

In my judgment, a covenant of three commitments is required.

1. Even in these difficult times, society must commit resources sufficient to attract talented individuals to these institutions—as both students and teachers. It is not ordained that universities and their faculties be always richly endowed, but resources consistent with their role and mission are an absolute necessity.

2. Society must continue to preserve the university's essential freedom to remain a critic of existing arrangements—whether in science or society. Our future depends even more on freedom preserved than on full funding retained. New knowledge does not always require funds, but it does require freedom to determine the basic priorities of our critical investigations. This freedom is essentially an individual freedom, and we should not lose sight of the fact that at times academic freedom is threatened not only by forces external to the university, but by our colleagues among the students and faculty with little respect for views other than their own.

3. The university community must show evidence of a commitment to its tasks as well as a capacity to make difficult decisions that rise above purely parochial concerns, thereby demonstrating that it deserves such special responsibilities and treatment. Thus, the free exercise of reason, so essential to a university's life, cannot be confused with loose speculation. It must instead be associated with disciplined, unprejudiced testing of alternative ideas. Enlightenment does not emerge from the free association of emancipated minds at "rap sessions." The development of knowledge often proceeds in what may seem to be a wild and unpredictable way, driven by the powerful imaginations and impatient energies of creative investigators. In fact, however, it is given structure and direction by the disciplined use of reason in the evaluation of ideas, new and old.

If we in the university community are willing to use society's resources with discrimination and care and to rededicate ourselves to the truly important tasks facing us, the decade of the 1980s can be an opportunity gained—an opportunity to turn fully to the issues where we can make our greatest contribution. We cannot simply wish away the difficult sections of the road before us, but we must not allow the difficulties to govern our course. To quote Emerson: "This time like all times is a very good time if we but know what to do with it."

We recognize that society has other important needs, besides those represented by universities. There are needs in health, in energy, in the inner cities, in old-age security, and other important problems. To qualify for support in view of these other pressing and legitimate needs, we must demonstrate our capacity to actually perform the functions we speak so fondly of and not to be sidetracked to less worthy efforts. The 1980s will surely be a time of testing for us all.

It will require courage—by both faculties and legislators—to look to the preservation of the truly sustaining values of our society and the institutions that support them. It is difficult to rescue from our daily distractions the capacity to dedicate ourselves to the critical long-run concerns of society. The university, along with the fundamental ideas it embodies, is one of these concerns. I hope the community of scholars—both students and faculty—here at the University of Michigan will demonstrate that the university upholds its part of the covenant and is worthy of such special consideration.

The University of Michigan is preparing for the 1980s in an adventurous and optimistic mode. We are confident of our sense of community and our capacity to generate a considered response to the challenges ahead of us. We are completing new libraries and associated facilities to support our continuing commitment to scholarship. We expect, with the citizens of the state of Michigan, to build a great new medical center and have begun the development of new facilities for our College of Engineering. Most important of all, we are focusing our efforts on attracting and retaining outstanding faculty and students.

We do not intend to stand politely by and thus risk slipping backward during the coming decade. Rather, we eagerly face the challenge ahead of us and commit ourselves, in a spirit of both pride and humility, to do whatever it takes to maintain and enhance the distinction of our programs. We should be aware, however, that this effort will severely test our resolve, and perhaps even our sense of community. It is easy to talk of distinction, a challenge actually to attain it. In this effort, we will need the support of all the collaborators in our past successes—our sister institutions of higher learning, our alumni and friends, the citizens of the state of Michigan, and of course, our distinguished faculty, staff, and students. I have every confidence that we will succeed, and that the most exciting days of our long intellectual adventure lie ahead of us.

American Higher Education: A Special Tradition Faces a Special Challenge

The Challenge of Change

Over the last century American colleges and universities have been transformed from quiet centers of cultural orthodoxy—largely removed from the dynamic forces propelling our society forward—to institutions fully participating in the adaptive changes that have gained us a position of world leadership. If American higher education is to retain its vitality as a cultural institution, it will have to perpetuate this process of adaptation and change. As it does so, it must continue to serve the society that supports it as well as to preserve its own sustaining traditions and values.

Universities operate within and reflect a broader cultural milieu; they cannot remain static in a world of rapid change, lest they be quickly replaced by other, more adaptive institutions. Developments in science alone will transform the face of all science-related institutions that wish to remain viable in the next decades, for science has not only become an instrument of public policy but is advancing at an unprecedented pace. Furthermore, the distinction between basic and applied research is blurring, and the research agendas of all science-oriented institutions are becoming more interdependent. Other changes—the worldwide explosion of ideological fervor; the rapidly accelerating international movement of capital, technology, and production facilities; the information revolution; the disappearance of the world's peasantry and its institutions; the changing nature of family life in our society; the new professional roles being taken by women and minorities; the daily ironic confrontation between human discovery and human destruction—all these conspire to create a world in which sense and stability sometimes seem to have evaporated. In such a climate it is impossible for higher education to transmit values from one generation to another by simply employing the successful formulas of an earlier time. In this constantly shifting environment, universities must respond to the various challenges of change while simultaneously protecting themselves from the fervent but suspect ideologies that change inspires.

Mutation, change, and novelty are the most common phenomena in the universe. The challenge is to *select* from the innumerable novelties that are sure to confront us those few that will effectively transform our lives and institutions. In this age of information, it is only our power of perceptive selection and thoughtful preservation that can prevent the rising tide of information from overwhelming us. That is why this is such an exciting moment for higher education. Our nation's colleges and universities have developed a special capacity to engage in selective preservation and change. Indeed, at their best, they might, as Alfred North Whitehead recommended, help us "to preserve order amid change and to preserve change amid order."

Higher education has particular capacities and responsibilities in a rapidly shifting world. It is not itself the vehicle of change, but it can provide the ideas, tools, and concepts needed to select a new direction. In considering how we might meet the challenges of the next decades, I do not believe we can operate outside the enduring values and traditions of our own history. The status quo will prove inadequate, but ahistorical, utopian thinking will not bring us nearer to our goals. Before proceeding, it is thus necessary to weave a tapestry out of the educational traditions that have informed the evolution of American higher education—from the original colonial colleges to the great land-grant universities and "polytechnic" schools to contemporary liberal arts colleges and, most particularly, the modern research university.

The Sources of Our Traditions

Surprisingly perhaps, I will weave my tapestry in part from the Bible, beginning with passages from the Old Testament Book of Proverbs, moving to the twelfth-century biblical scholar and physician Maimonides, and concluding with an admonitory passage from the New Testament Gospel of Matthew. Not only is the Bible an important influence on our society and on the first universities, but it remains one of our greatest works of literature, whatever its source of revelation.

It may seem peculiar to reach back into the Old Testament for ideas and values that have informed the development of the modern university. After all, in the Book of Genesis the "tree of knowledge" is associated with the fall of humankind. But the Book of Proverbs, composed much later (100 B.C.) than Genesis, belongs to a series of Old Testament writings reflecting on the nature of social and moral experience. Sometimes known as "The Wise Sayings of Solomon," it incorporates some wise advice about education into its stated objectives:

- for education in wisdom and moral discipline,
- for the understanding of thoughtful speech,
- for training in the discernment of what is right and proper and ethical,
- to sharpen the wit of the ignorant,
- to give knowledge and foresight.

Clearly, the principles of a liberal education predate the earliest universities by over a millennium. The Book of Proverbs goes on to extol the benefits of the earnest search for wisdom, as well as the security and obligation of scholars. The wisdom in the Book of Proverbs can best be described as an ethical wisdom, whose source is not human reason but God, and whose object is not insight into life or the universe but moral behavior. This view is shared by such prophets as Isaiah, who disparage mortal erudition: "The wisdom of their wise men shall perish, and the knowledge of their knowledgeable men shall be hidden" (Isaiah 29:14).

Proverbs is especially suited to our purposes because its author(s) were not dominated by priestly and prophetic interests but by the desire to interpret religious and social practices. They represent a kind of independent force in the social and cultural life of their period. In this sense, as we shall see, they share a common heritage with the founders of the very first universities.

While the concept of wisdom espoused in the Book of Proverbs differs fundamentally from that held by college faculties today, these biblical notions were hardly foreign to those who, in the eleventh and twelfth centuries, established the first universities at Oxford, Cambridge, Paris, Montpellier, Toulouse, Salerno, Bologna, Heidelberg, Cologne, Cracow, and Prague. Scholars, students, and patrons of these universities placed their efforts firmly within an ecclesiastic framework. The University of Cracow, for instance, was founded in 1364 by Casimir the Great "for the conversion of heathens . . . and a greater ordering of the Catholic faith." More typical of the ideas that shaped the earliest universities, however, is Maimonides's prayer:

> Be thou with me almighty Father in all my efforts—may there never rise in me the notion that I know enough, but give me strength—to enlarge my knowledge. Our world is great and the mind of man presses forward forever—guide us in the immense work so that I may be of avail.

This passage strikingly captures the Augustinian notion that humanity could participate in the improvement of its own condition and understanding—a capacity only hinted at in the Book of Proverbs. Although the Almighty remained the ultimate controlling force in our destiny, the human mind played an ever greater part. This new concept of the human role in the divine unfolding of history was a crucial step in enabling the idea of a university.

In this new environment wisdom and learning could represent an independent force in society. Even the University of Cracow, founded by royal charter, was allotted a limited autonomy and independence in order to perform its tasks. It began with chairs in civil (Roman) law, the liberal arts, and medicine, in addition to positions in canon law.

The earliest universities were not even institutions as such. Instead, informal groups of students and scholars—*universitas* (a group of persons)—came together to study matters of mutual interest. This wonderfully unfettered form of association, however, lasted only a few years. Thereafter these small mobile groups rapidly took on the characteristics of institutions. In southern Europe this transformation was forced by students, who demanded accountability for the quality of teaching. In northern Europe the faculty was seeking protection from ecclesiastical or political authorities, which quickly came to dominate them in spite of these efforts.

Two particular traits of these early medieval universities

deeply influenced their modern-day successors. First, the brief early period of unfettered independence continued to capture the imagination of scholars and students. Some kind of special independence would remain essential to the vigor of all Western universities, even though society would not always permit it. Second, the earliest curricula included the professions (theology, law, and medicine) as well as the arts. Contemporary observers who decry the increased "vocationalism" of our universities are thus working from incorrect assumptions. Professional education has been part of university life from the beginning.

Despite a promising start, the medieval university mainly served the existing establishment, remained firmly rooted in the status quo, and fostered few new ideas. The many sparkling developments of medieval science, as well as the enormous strides of the Renaissance and Enlightenment, largely bypassed the university. There were, of course, some notable exceptions like Sir Isaac Newton, but during the long period between the thirteenth and the nineteenth centuries, other institutions—certain guild schools, science academies, even religious brotherhoods—became society's chief instruments of discovery and change. Universities sank into a long period of quasi hibernation. But the early, transient spark of independence—first lit in the later books of the Old Testament and fanned by St. Augustine and other Christian scholars—did not die out. It remained a flame in the Western imagination, to be rekindled in more recent times.

The Beginnings of Higher Education in America

In the middle of the long period of quasi hibernation for European universities, the first American colleges took shape. They were established not by independent groups of faculty and students but rather by local communities wishing to ensure a literate clergy and an adequate pool of public servants. Their responsibility to an external community, public or private, is the first of the distinctive American traditions in higher education. It is historically inaccurate to picture the American university as isolated from the surrounding community in a completely disinterested quest for knowledge.

During the seventeenth, eighteenth, and nineteenth centuries

American colleges and universities, like their European counterparts of the time, were conceived and operated as pillars of the locally established church or political order, and their curricula were designed to reflect and perpetuate contemporary social values and institutional arrangements. Unfortunately, these early American institutions were not pillars of either education or scholarship. On the contrary, their presidents were often the only staff members with adequate training and experience, and even that was sometimes marginal.

These colleges, however, did not aspire to explore fresh ideas. Neither the faculty nor the students strove for new insight into the nature of human experience or the universe. They concentrated instead on reinforcing the various cultural traditions that they served. Academic freedom as we know it was not intended or even considered. Colleges aimed to preserve knowledge and promote morality; new values and new arrangements in science and society had to be sought elsewhere. In those early days of a weak academic guild and an uninvolved federal government, universities were dominated by their presidents and lay governing boards. The faculty had little influence or prestige.

The Enlightenment Reaches the University

Higher education began to change radically in the nineteenth century. In Europe the hold of ecclesiastical authorities on the universities and their faculties had been broken earlier, only to be replaced by the control of the central government—a situation that, to some extent, persists to this day. Nevertheless, in early nineteenth-century Germany, Enlightenment ideas began to penetrate institutions of higher education. The first step toward modern academic freedom in these universities was gaining the "privilege" to discuss alternative, unorthodox theological ideas. This is not so far from the Book of Proverbs after all. It is, however, noteworthy that this privilege was at first restricted to discussions taking place *on campus.* Thus the ivory tower was constructed as much to wall academics in as to keep the community out.

Once these seeds of academic freedom were sown, they soon spread to other areas, both inside and outside the university. German universities first fully developed the notion that the university was the appropriate place to foster new ideas of all kinds—in science as well as theology—along with the training of a new generation of students. British universities also began to revitalize themselves, focusing especially on the education of undergraduates in residential settings. Slowly they too started to introduce training and research in science, engineering, and the development of new technology. Authority and power in these universities was gradually transferred from the governing boards and president to the faculty.

It is hard to overestimate the far-reaching consequences of these changes. The modern Western university, devoted to education in the context of a constantly renewed search for new ideas and understandings, is a unique achievement of our civilization. In many ways this educational revolution was the latest of the great liberal revolutions of the Enlightenment, based on that set of ideas which began transforming most Western institutions in the eighteenth century: faith in the primacy of reason and cognition, in the potential for progress, and in the importance of individual rights and human dignity. Above all, new limits were placed on the power of the state by the recognition of the individual as the ultimate source of the state's legitimacy.

Thus, the Western academic world emerged, as did Western economies and nation-states, as a kind of spontaneous order operating on the principle of competitive collaboration. That is, the entire system was driven by a concept of competitive excellence based on intellectual objectivity and independence. In scholarship we came to believe that truth would inevitably vanquish prejudice and falsehood, just as in the Western economic and political order less viable institutional arrangements are driven out of the "market" by more viable ones.

In the contemporary Western world the primacy of reason, cognition, and the pursuit of knowledge are the foundations of our intellectually and scientifically based culture. The obligations and prerogatives of the modern university follow from its central cultural purpose as the focus of society's efforts to develop new understandings on the basis of reason. Our commitment to rationality and our desire for new knowledge are not produced by the university; rather, the modern university is itself produced by them.

Developments in Nineteenth- and Twentieth-Century America

Certain strands of this evolving tapestry of modern higher education are traceable to events in nineteenth-century America. With the enormous expansion westward came the establishment of hundreds of new colleges, designed to serve their communities in much the same way as the earlier colonial colleges had served theirs. But change was also in the air. During the latter half of the nineteenth century educational leaders such as Tappan and Angell at the University of Michigan and Eliot at Harvard began to fashion institutions similar to the research universities being established in Germany. They also incorporated many aspects of the British system, with its emphasis on undergraduate education—including the cultivation of a moral sense—in a residential setting. Despite this educational leadership, elite colleges and universities long neglected modern science, particularly experimental science, in part because of their aversion to practical training. At these institutions science first entered the curriculum as natural philosophy.

During this period the initiative, imagination, and leadership in higher education lay elsewhere. The Morrill Act, the land-grant universities, and the engineering-oriented "polytechnic" schools took the lead in bringing experimental science into American universities. More importantly, these developments established two new and distinctly American traditions. First, higher education became broadly involved in training professionals, as well as augmenting and preserving the knowledge base necessary to such training. The curriculum was dramatically expanded in order to serve society's rapidly growing needs and to train the "ordinary" citizen in the "agricultural and mechanical arts." Second, higher education was no longer reserved to ministers, public servants, and the intellectual elite. Instead, a special tradition of access made it increasingly available to a broad spectrum of Americans wishing to gain expertise in a wide variety of areas and professions.

By the turn of the century, therefore, the modern profile of American colleges and universities had begun to take shape. Although the system continued to evolve throughout the first half of the twentieth century, the next series of major changes did not occur until after World War II. Interestingly, these transformations were driven by a sequence of new resource commitments on the part of the federal government. In the immediate post-war period, the GI Bill offered federal support to veterans desiring further education. Moreover, between 1945 and 1965, a series of federal initiatives began funding university-based research. These actions, which largely defined the present status of the nation's research universities, account for the current intimate coupling of education and research at these institutions—a distinctly American model. Also distinctly American is the central and indispensable role the university plays in the national research and development effort. There was one less fortunate side effect. This generous financial support of university research suggested—incorrectly and counterproductively—that the academic research agenda could be completely divorced from other research efforts in our society.

By 1965 the tradition of federal support for higher education in the United States had become an integral part of academic life. Finally, beginning in 1965, a series of federal initiatives in the area of student financial aid began to address more fully the issue of equitable access to the nation's universities.

By way of summary, let me highlight six distinctively American traditions that have emerged from the history of higher education and that fundamentally shape our present-day colleges and universities. First, our faculties and students are responsible to some external community, whether public or private. As a result, their relationships to other groups and institutions in society have always been broader, better established, and more natural than those of their European counterparts.

Second, American higher education is decentralized, and its institutions vary in size, purpose, and organization. This heterogeneity reflects our history, our pluralistic society, and the variety of educational and other needs that must be met by higher education. As so often in the United States, we celebrate the heterogeneity of our system, pointing to these differences as a source of strength and vitality. We also believe that, as in other sectors of our society, a kind of "unseen hand" guides the development of the entire enterprise so that there is, in fact, a competitive collaboration at work within it.

Third, the educational and research programs of American colleges and universities serve an unusually wide spectrum of society's needs for highly trained personnel and the knowledge underlying this training. Thus they pursue learning for its own sake, preserve and pass on what we believe to be of enduring value in our culture, and transfer—directly or indirectly—socially useful new ideas in science, technology, and the study of the human condition.

Fourth, American universities serve a dual role as both society's servant and society's critic. On the one hand, higher education is responsible for the training and research functions that serve society's economic and cultural life. On the other hand, the university community has the additional obligation to criticize society's current arrangements and values as well as construct, entertain, and test alternative visions of our institutions and alternative approaches to understanding nature. Society's support for this dual endeavor is sustained by faith in human rationality, knowledge, science, and progress. Despite such faith, the relationship between patron and critic is inevitably uneasy. But such uneasiness is far better than the irrelevance of universities in earlier years.

Fifth, although American institutions of higher education are responsible to various external governing bodies, the emergence of the tradition of academic freedom during this century has shifted power and independence from the central administration and external trustees to the faculty. The university may now, however, have relinquished considerable power and authority to government and other interests because of its dependence on these sources for support. This trend differs from the early days of surrender to external religious, moral, or political standards, but it may determine, directly or indirectly, what the faculty "choose" to study and what type of education is available to students.

Sixth, American colleges and universities are extraordinarily accessible to the nation's pool of appropriately qualified and motivated students. Nevertheless, our full obligations in this arena have yet to be met.

These six characteristics define the essential aspects of American higher education today. Predictably, we have in some ways preserved and in others transformed the long history we inherited. My purpose in reflecting on the roots and informing values of our current system is to enable us more effectively to consider the question of how we might best meet the challenges of the next decades.

The Responsibilities of the Contemporary University

Thus we arrive at the mid-1980s, a time when the American system of higher education, despite its deficiencies, is the envy of the world. It remains a vast, unplanned, largely uncoordinated effort that produces a wide variety of socially useful outcomes. Although it is supported by a huge array of patrons with sometimes conflicting goals, most of these patrons seem to appreciate the social value of a university system that is both responsible and independent.

The principles governing the special privileges and responsibilities of the university are intellectual autonomy, broad political and philosophic neutrality, and academic freedom. Correspondingly, the university is obligated to serve society's need for advanced education, to develop new knowledge and insight, and to aid in the process of selective preservation and change. Critical to this role is the capacity for independence, reflection, and ongoing appraisal of society's efforts, constrained only by the use of reason. Importantly, the modern university is not an instrument for solving society's problems but a repository of the tools, the language, and some of the alternative visions needed to explore new solutions. It is a resource for change, but it cannot sponsor particular movements without undermining its defining characteristic as an independent source of ideas.

The face of American life will take on a strikingly altered aspect in the next decades. We will participate in a world economic and political community whose members are increasingly interdependent and in which no single power can be economically, politically, or militarily dominant. Science and technology will play an expanding role in both the marketplace and national security. The pace of scientific progress will require closer interaction between institutions primarily engaged in basic science and those engaged in applied research and development. An ever more diverse American society will demand new insights and commitments to ensure our future as a pluralistic democracy. In such an environment, an institution dedicated to selective preservation and change, as well as committed to our national effort in research and development, can and should take a central part in our national life. Indeed, in any prescription for continued world leadership by the United States, the strength and vitality of its universities is an essential ingredient.

As we confront the challenges of our future, we must attend especially to our responsibility for selective preservation. Our society's traditional values can continue to provide an anchor for our future efforts, ensuring that we are not buffeted in all directions at once by the winds of change. The age of tolerance ushered in by the ideals of the Enlightenment could yield a bitter harvest if we permit ourselves to regard all values as equally acceptable and thus deny the existence of any absolute values. Contemporary higher education, precisely because it is such an important locus of change, must also take the lead in exploring, explicating, and reinforcing those values that we hold essential to the ultimate vitality and humaneness of our society. We must, in the end, sustain our belief and identity as a society. It is the university's special role not only to help in this endeavor but to prevent intolerance of new ideas and to promote judiciousness in the social regulation of behavior. Universities must also take the lead in ensuring a fair hearing for opposing views and in imparting the necessity of compromise for the health of our democratic society.

I turn now, as promised, to the Gospel of Matthew. In Matthew 25, one of the Parables of the Kingdom called the Parable of the Journeying Property Owner features a certain master who, before departing on a lengthy journey, entrusts each of his servants with a certain amount of his capital, or "talents." In earliest time, "talents" were a unit of weight; they later became a unit of monetary value, and finally, a measure of human capacity. Some of the servants used this capital wisely and caused it to grow. From these productive activities came the famous saying, "Give me five talents, and I will give you five talents more." Others, however, simply "buried their talents in the ground," returning intact only the original sum. The moral, of course, is that we are obligated to use the capacities we have and the assets entrusted to us productively. In a messianic community, this message carried a more ominous undertone, namely, that we would all be held to account for our efforts in the "day of days."

But this message is singularly appropriate for leaders of today's colleges and universities as well. It is our obligation to build upon the "talents"—in the contemporary sense—of the students we accept for further study. In the next decades, as higher and higher proportions of minorities join our labor force, we will need to become more sensitive to the needs of these populations, which have been historically underserved by and underrepresented within higher education. We can never adequately respond to our obligation to nurture the talents of our society without more effectively meeting our obligations to minorities. Just as the parable speaks of holding individuals to account for their efforts, so colleges and universities can expect to be held to account by a society that has entrusted us with some of its most valuable capital.

To ensure an adequate return on society's investment in them, American institutions of higher education have at least the following responsibilities:

- to define their objectives carefully and selectively;
- to evaluate all possible means for improving the productivity of their administrative and academic activities;
- to review the quality and centrality of their various programs carefully and honestly;
- to set priorities among their objectives;
- to recognize that all institutions evolve over time and that no existing arrangement should be exempt from reexamination;
- to consider new institutional arrangements that counteract the concerns often raised by the narrow disciplinary focus of the overall research university;
- to develop a policy for providing access to qualified, motivated, but underrepresented minorities;
- to continue to fashion appropriate links with other institutions.

If we illuminate the road before us and can respond thoughtfully and effectively to our rapidly changing environment, we can continue to play a critical role in our society's evolution.

Higher education must understand its obligations to society, but society must also understand its obligation to sustain the particular set of conditions necessary for colleges and universities to perform their functions. It will not do for government to react in a threatening and intimidating manner every time college and university faculties or students fault the status quo. If we do not have faith in our capacity to sift emergent ideas, we will lose our ability to develop new ideas altogether. It is time to restore our faith in human reason, to give it the opportunity to explore new avenues for the challenges that lie ahead. This is the modern American tradition in higher education and it can serve us well in the climate that will face the next generation.

The Modern Research University

Higher education, whether in the United States or in Europe, has not always ranked research as a primary element of its mission. Beginning perhaps with the first federal research grant to the Franklin Institute more than 150 years ago, American colleges and universities have slowly strengthened their commitment in this area. In the late nineteenth century our growing national desire to participate in new economic and scientific enterprises led American educators and public officials to begin emulating the scientific and technical capacity of the German university. It was then that some colleges and universities made their first efforts to integrate the scholarly with the teaching function.

Not until after World War II, however, did research become a central activity in American institutions of higher education. At that time, the United States converted a large military research enterprise into a peacetime effort, based for the most part at universities and allocated through a peer review system. Not only has research now become a crucial function of American colleges and universities; it has also become symbiotically related to advanced training and essential to the intellectual, economic, technological, and military health of the nation.

In the United States, then, the close connection between higher education and research is only about half a century old. So it is in no way ordained that universities and their faculties must always occupy the role in society that we associate today with the research university. Indeed, basic transformations in the entire structure of our national research and development effort may eventually require the research university to play a somewhat different role than it does today. But for the present the great research universities remain dedicated to general and professional education, to advanced research training, and to the development of new knowledge.

Every such scholarly community rests ultimately on a deep

and abiding belief in the products of the intellect. As scholars, we share a commitment to pursuing knowledge and cultivating reason in ourselves and in others. Moreover, as a cultural institution, the contemporary university is a product of society's belief in the primacy of reason and cognition. Since universities take their mandate from the society around them, our scholarly and other creative efforts must, sooner or later, clarify problems that affect society as a whole. The future vitality of scholarship at our universities depends not only on our own creative abilities but also on the attitude of society toward knowledge, understanding, and the prospects for human development.

Unfortunately, at this historical moment, many in our society are skeptical about the impact of new knowledge and scientific progress on the quality of human life. They doubt the simple notion that the advance of knowledge is a form of pure light liberating us from the darkness of ignorance. In fact, some believe that the march of science works to submerge our true human nature and thus prevents us from addressing the most important problems of human existence. In addition, many resist what they consider the suffocating impact of Western rationalism, which they feel undermines a certain conception of human dignity based on love and individual spontaneity. Although I believe such attitudes to be mistaken, it is only fair to note that those who are abandoning the idea of "progress through reason" are legitimately responding to certain massive human failures of recent decades—to say nothing of the laws of thermodynamics. A middle-ground position would posit reason and the development of knowledge as key strategies in molding a better human existence, but would also acknowledge them as strategies that are unlikely to answer all the great questions of human life and its prospects for the future.

My own view of reason is pragmatic, straightforward, and I hope not too naive. Despite both the disappointments that regularly mar our history and the obstacles to a more ordered universe posed by the laws of thermodynamics, I decline either to succumb to considerations of increased entropy or to take refuge in irrational faiths. The work of the research university has, I believe, intrinsic merit because knowledge, reason, and scientific progress continue to be among the great humanizing and liberalizing forces in our culture. It is, therefore, the distinct privilege of university communities to protect and sustain these forces, secure in the knowledge of their ultimate significance.

In my view, humankind is moving toward a destination which, although imperfectly foreseeable, can be a better place than the one we now occupy. Importantly for the scholarly community, our ability both to discern and to reach such a destination depends in part on our capacity to generate new knowledge. This general outlook, I am convinced, is not necessarily incompatible with a view of the universe as, to some extent, random and chaotic. In the end, however, I prefer the "Ramsey approach," namely, that complete disorder is an impossibility.

In fact, for a scholarly community this view has few satisfactory alternatives. The difficulties of alternative views can be illustrated by recalling the basic tenets of the modernist movement in art and other aspects of twentieth-century cultural life. One objective of this movement, as I understand it, was to liberate our imaginations from the yoke of the past—in particular, from the concept of the so-called rational man. The alternative the modernists proposed, however, was to conceive of the world as a random succession of stimuli to which we respond, if at all, with passive receptivity. In such an environment, concern with the self and its various psychic states seems to overshadow any attempt to "order" our outer reality. Although such movements have undoubtedly enhanced our understanding of the human condition, as well as satisfying other human needs, it is difficult to imagine a productive community of scholars in an atmosphere suffused with such ideas. The long-range prospects for both scholars and scholarship depend, in part, on society's and our own evaluation of taking a rational approach to the challenges of human existence.

Despite contrary voices, in the short run we find ourselves in a public context congenial to the scholarly approach and the development of new knowledge. Indeed, the 1980s show some promise of a heightened societal interest in new knowledge of all kinds. The world, however, constantly changes, and the world of scholarship must change with it. If universities wish to participate fully in these developments, we must remain flexible and adaptable without compromising our fundamental obligations to scholarship and society.

In order to make judicious decisions about new directions for the research university to take, it is important to understand some of its chief sociocultural characteristics as they have emerged in recent decades. Let me therefore cite five general issues that affect the structure and role of research universities today.

First, all universities operate within and reflect a broader cultural milieu. In many ways the contemporary Western university is a natural outgrowth and a particular achievement of the Western liberal democracies and can now be viewed as one of their prototypical institutions. Despite their unique elements, special privileges, and particular responsibilities, universities reflect many of the assumptions, values, and organizational patterns common to Western democratic societies.

Our academic communities also exhibit many of the productive tensions that characterize other sectors of our society. The scholarly arena, for instance, is at once fiercely competitive and strongly cooperative. In the academic and political subcultures of our society, the characteristics of individuality and competition, on the one hand, and cooperation, on the other, often produce tensions that must be resolved before productive work can occur. In both the political and the academic sphere, these tensions result in a kind of skepticism about the status quo, which translates into the critical vitality and willingness to change that so importantly inform contemporary life, both within and without academia.

In other ways universities resemble the economic sector. Like our economic system, the contemporary academic world has no overall plan but nevertheless produces socially useful outcomes. Although a superficial anarchy seems to distinguish the structure of our national economy and our national academic enterprise, they are both, in fact, models of competitive cooperation. While the optimal balance of these forces is quite different in these two sectors and is achieved in quite different ways, in both our economic and our academic systems the pursuit of excellence and individual achievement drives the system forward and defines a framework for moving toward other objectives. A great university must, on the one hand, enable its members to compete in pursuing excellence, to be highly independent and individualistic, and to be committed to the discipline of an intellectual life. On the other hand, it must create an environment in which knowledge is shared through teaching and collaboration and in which an aura of collegiality nourishes the academic community as a whole.

Our society and its values are not, of course, in static equilibrium. We continue to grapple with such issues as equality and inequality, as well as with the appropriate balance between individual incentives and rewards versus communal and social motivations and with the balance between our national versus our international obligations. The outcome of these ongoing debates is certain to affect the future structure and role of our academic communities. Our part in these debates is to ensure that our faculty and students conduct thoughtful and creative conversations on topics that really matter.

A second issue is the intimate relationship within American universities of the teaching and research programs. Most American educators believe that while this close link may not be absolutely necessary, it is largely responsible for the current world leadership of the United States in science and technology. Many observers contend that this strong association between university-based research and educational programs significantly enhances both the production of a skilled labor force—especially in the area of advanced research training—and the development of research. Thus it is doubly critical that we nurture our university-based research efforts since they also contribute importantly to the training of young students and scholars.

Third, our universities must be at once responsive to society's needs and independent enough to reformulate the great human problems and the solutions to them when necessary. The contemporary research university interacts more and more with external institutions, including other universities, and so must consciously construct mechanisms to preserve its critical independence from them and its own special sense of community. There is a dynamic tension between our attempts to harvest the fruits of such intermural interactions and our efforts to protect the scholarly agenda and independence of our own community. In the current era of rapid change, this tension is perfectly natural.

The sponsorship and application of new scholarship compel universities to interact with larger social, political, and economic forces, which in turn affect both the environment within which scholarship takes shape and the scholarly agenda itself. For example, post–World War II science policy, which developed out of the strategic competition between the superpowers, has strikingly influenced the scientific programs of academia. As a consequence, we find ourselves at a special moment in the evolution of science and the role of science in our society. In the United States, university-based science is a critical part of the national research and development effort, which has for the first time become an instrument of national policy. Thus our responsibilities to the university must be constantly balanced against our obligations to our country, especially in an era of changing demographics, federal deficits, and increased competition from alternative research organizations both here and abroad.

In addition, the values and objectives of each individual institution involved in the conservation, production, and utilization of knowledge influence the entire enterprise. For example, developments in university-based research alter the structure of disciplines and educational programs within universities, as well as affecting other organizations that collaborate with us or use our products and services.

Thus, from without and from within, the modern research university faces changes that will inevitably cause faculty, students, and administrators to reassess academic norms, structures, and overall goals. In evaluating the prospects for our research universities, therefore, we must be more cognizant than ever of the permeable membrane separating the academic community from, and connecting it to, the society around it.

A fourth set of issues concerns the simultaneous diversity and intensity of scholarship carried out by research universities. The depth of specialization represented in university faculties is part of their greatness. But the relentless increase in the specialization of academic disciplines, the steady growth in interaction between each university and other academic and nonacademic institutions, and the rising demand for universities to assume additional roles and tasks have set up dangerous centrifugal forces within individual academic communities. These forces could pull many academic activities to the periphery and thus undermine the essential community of interest so necessary to the life of our universities as we know them.

Only a thoughtful and vigilant commitment to preserving individual academic communities will prevent the various disciplines from moving outward, leaving no solid core to sustain our common life. To counteract this tendency, we must become "politicians"—in the root sense of building the *polis* or community. As Bart Giamatti, former president of Yale University, once told his colleagues,

> The shape of a university depends finally on how the people within it treat one another and perceive each other as engaged in a common enterprise regardless of potentially divisive differences of background or philosophical point of view. The shape [of a university] depends on that intangible quality of collegiality upon which all other forms of quality . . . depend.

This is not an exhortation to return to an earlier time, but rather a call to foster those values that I believe will sustain the foundations of our teaching and scholarship for the future.

Fifth, and perhaps most important, research universities must establish a supportive and stimulating environment for scholarship, inspiring pride and satisfaction in the roles of scholar, teacher, researcher, student, and support staff. Any institution as complex as a modern research university evokes many kinds of reactions, even within a single academic community. Its faculty, staff, and students alternatively love and hate it, praise and damn it, defend and attack it, preserve and try to change it. Life in such a setting is, to say the least, exciting. Yet the deepest excitement of university life comes from the opportunity to participate in new ideas and discoveries, to communicate with clarity and expertise, and to improve the society in which we live. It is this excitement that cements our loyalty to the research university even through the sacrifice of difficult times.

In the final analysis we must demonstrate to society that scholars and scholarship speak to the vital problems of human existence, at least to those that are tractable. In fulfilling this function successfully, we assure a future for the research university.

Managing Research Institutions under Resource Constraints

Key Issues

1. There has never been enough money to satisfy the legitimate aspirations of a truly enterprising faculty or administration.
2. Optimal strategies for the deployment of university resources will depend on our beliefs about the central goals and values of the university. In addition, they will be institution specific and difficult to locate.
3. The research university is involved in the production (creation) of joint products. A neat separation of its efforts in education and scholarship is not possible without fundamentally transforming the institution. The American research university is an integrated and synergistic set of activities and must be considered as a unified entity. Failure to do so will inevitably undermine the institution as we know it. Changing levels of resource commitments from any of its many patrons and/or partners will affect both education and scholarship.
4. The cost of quality in education and scholarship will probably rise faster than the total resource base of most research universities.
5. Solutions (strategies) available to a single institution may not be available to the research university system as a whole. Both individual and national strategies are therefore required.
6. The status quo is never quite right. The difficult challenge is to select the change—however large or small—that moves us closer to society's long-run needs.

In the early 1980s the University of Michigan faced declining support from one of its chief patrons, the state of Michigan. Since

139

the activities of all research universities are complexly interrelated, I believe that diminished support from any patron at any research university forces a similar set of issues to the surface. The first-round effects, the relative impact, and the available solutions may differ from one university to another, but if the change in support levels persists, the set of issues confronted will be remarkably similar. I hope my experiences at the University of Michigan—both the successes and the failures—can be useful to those who find themselves in comparable circumstances at other institutions.

Some General Strategies

If "constraints" were to be defined merely as "perceived limitations," then resource constraints could be said to characterize the entire history of higher education. There has never been enough money to satisfy the legitimate aspirations of a truly enterprising faculty or administration. In a dynamic environment any research university with a genuine commitment to deploying and redeploying its assets in the most effective possible way continuously faces difficult resource allocation decisions. This is especially true when, as today, the cost of quality in education and scholarship rises faster than the total resource base of most research universities. In some respects, therefore, this latest challenge should present few qualitatively new types of decisions. Unfortunately, few of us have pursued our obligations with such constant vigilance as to be able to claim that we have used our existing resource base to maximum effect.

In any case, it is probably more useful—and more timely—to think of "resource constraints" as alluding to the potential for a sharp and possibly broad decline in the patronage of this nation's research universities. At the current time, for example, there is widespread concern about continuing federal support for research funding, student aid, medical science, and medical education, as well as the impact of tax reform on the revenues of universities. Cumulatively, all these changes could significantly affect the quality of, and access to, the contemporary American research university. In addition, many state universities fear loss of substantial support from state governments. Whatever the source of the prospective limitation, for present purposes I take "resource constraints" to refer to any situation in which the academic community believes that the real resources (e.g., faculty, facilities) available from traditional sources for future deployment will not support the desired level and quality of activity. However straightforward the predicament, we must consider a number of complex, interrelated factors in order to devise appropriate strategies for coping with it. Let me highlight a few.

First, we must understand the university as a dynamic system. Since every institution is embedded in its own unique history, the availability and deployment of resources—both human and physical, tangible and intangible—must be viewed as outcomes of processes evolving through time, often extensive periods of time. The natural life cycle of any substantial academic initiative, for example, should probably be measured in decades, especially if the entire community is trying to adjust to it simultaneously. As any biologist, economist, or electrical engineer can attest, the behavioral characteristics of a dynamic system are much more complex than those of a static system. In particular, we cannot always trust our intuition in solving a complex, time-dependent problem with many interdependent feedback loops. Optimal solutions in such cases can have surprising features.

Second, as in any dynamic system, we are confronted with a complex cluster of interrelated issues. In locating the set of feasible and then optimal solutions, each institution must consider *at least* the following seven factors.

1. *Initial conditions.* What is the current situation of the university and how did it get there? At present, for instance, most universities will face new shortfalls with already depleted infrastructures (e.g., facilities, numbers of graduate students). This situation severely limits our options. Similarly, alternatives available when federal student aid support is rising, as it was between 1978 and 1982, are not available when it is falling.

Moreover, we must consider not only the spectrum and quality of current university activities but the relationship of these endeavors to the institution's goals and aspirations. In particular, it will be vital to assess both where an institution stands in relation to its objectives and whether it has been moving closer to or further from them. If, for example, an institution feels its current resources are optimally deployed to bring it nearer its goals, simple "across-the-board" adjustments might be the best policy.

2. *Uncertainties.* We must try to forecast future developments over which we may have little or no control. Appropriate solutions are unlikely to be formulated by optimizing over a period so short that all relevant variables are known. Particularly critical are the expected time profiles of resource availability (revenues) and costs. Equally crucial are judgments about the nature of education and scholarship in the future. In the area of research, for example, we must not only project the optimal combination of human and physical capital required to meet the challenges of the next decade; we must also compare the reproduction time for new human and physical capital. Here, as in many other life circumstances, we come up against the Kierkegaardian condition that "life must be understood backwards. But . . . it must be lived forwards."

3. *Balancing the budget.* In most cases, balancing the budget is a trivial matter. It may be more difficult to balance the budget while maintaining the institution's capacity to meet its various objectives over time. The best long-range adjustment may require running a temporary deficit.

4. *Flexibility.* Flexibility represents the capacity of an institution to reallocate resources within a relevant time frame. Any institution's response time will be affected by such factors as: the tenure and age profile of its faculty, the nature of its traditional and legal decision-making process, the distribution of its resources between physical and human capital. How much flexibility a given institution has in these areas can critically affect which strategies it prefers. In addition, the amount of flexibility available to a single institution differs from what is available to the research university system as a whole. So we must consider both individual and national strategies.

The collegial strength and decision-making tradition of the particular academic community may also largely determine which solutions are feasible. Each university has somewhat different traditions in the area of collegial decision making and governance, but I cannot resist recalling at this point a statement attributed to a well-known college president: "How can I democratize this college unless I have absolute authority?"

5. *Commitment, communication, morale.* Although each university may define a somewhat different community for itself, its long-term viability requires a joint and serious commitment of its

members—faculty, staff, and students—to a common vision. The moment when an institution is adjusting to new resource constraints, however, will normally be a time of unequal sacrifices, which can produce serious tensions. Such tensions can only be overcome by a sense of history and joint commitment to the university's future. To reinforce such commitment, accurate and timely communication is essential. Obstacles to be surmounted here are the unwillingness of faculties to read missives from administrators and the decreasing loyalty of students and faculty to their local academic communities as they strengthen ties to their disciplinary colleagues at other locations.

6. *Principles and practice.* Everyone favors selective budget cuts in principle. The idea of reallocating limited resources to areas of greatest merit rather than "mindlessly" cutting across the board meets with great enthusiasm at most faculty meetings. This attitude, of course, reveals that no one believes existing resources have been optimally deployed in the first place. If they had been, across-the-board cuts would be logical. I would, however, issue two warnings with respect to selective budget cuts. First, such cuts must be based on as much detailed information as possible, including a carefully and operationally articulated view of the institution's comparative strengths. Second, in practice a policy of selective budget cuts tends to isolate particular groups and, understandably, they fight back hard. The ensuing "discussion" can be heated and demoralizing, with those who contest the decision often attacking the more vulnerable process of decision making. In such an uneasy environment, it is necessary to remain focused on long-term needs and adhere strongly to one's convictions. To complicate matters further, if faculty groups are directly involved in deciding what to cut, serious dissension within the faculty itself may result. Thus, direct faculty involvement in the reallocation process has both advantages and disadvantages.

7. *Equity, fairness, efficiency.* It is always challenging to balance our responsibility for the efficient use of resources against appropriate concerns for equity and fairness. The latter issues affect the future vitality of a scholarly community as much as the more tractable issue of efficient resource deployment. The social fabric of a university or college, once rent, is difficult if not impossible to mend.

Third, we have only an approximate idea of what economists would call the "production function" of a university. That is, the relationship between various combinations of inputs (e.g., faculty, students, facilities) and the resulting outputs (e.g, education, scholarship, service) is only dimly understood.

Finally, the external environment within which any adjustment is contemplated will strongly affect institutional possibilities. Such external circumstances include the shifting demographics of the national population, changing social and political attitudes, the quality of primary and secondary schools, government finances, and economic conditions. With respect to government financing, the way we respond to changes in federal support for university-based research will depend on federal policy in such other areas as student aid, national laboratories, and tax reform. It is the cumulative impact of these policies that we must address.

All these factors merely represent themes in the complex counterpoint of issues at any individual institution. Clearly, however, successful strategies require us to solve a complex equation that relates conditions stemming from our institutional history to our present and future objectives and the resources we expect to have available to meet them. Adjusting any component of this multidimensional, time-dependent problem affects the whole. To such a task, no simple recipe is adequate, whether "smaller but better," "bigger is better," or "status quo is best." Yet universities must continue to take responsibility for their own future. Even in difficult circumstances, an academic community must summon the necessary will and energy to defend its crucial role as a center of critical inquiry and learning.

The University of Michigan: A Case Study

As a large state-assisted institution, the University of Michigan has major commitments in the areas of undergraduate and graduate education, professional education, advanced research training, and scholarship. In 1981–82 the Ann Arbor campus enrolled about 35,000 students, almost all full-time and about two-thirds undergraduates. In total we had approximately 4,500 instructional staff, 2,800 of whom were full-time faculty members. The remainder were graduate student teaching assistants. The state of Michigan supplied about 50 percent of the finances for our core instructional and re-search budgets, although this state support accounted for only 18 percent of the total university budget.[1]

Over the decade preceding 1982, the university's General Fund budget—financing our core programs—declined in terms of real re-sources on an average of 1 percent per year. Direct operating support from the state of Michigan dropped considerably further. Between 1972–73 and 1981–82, inflation-adjusted state support fell by an average of 3.2 percent a year. But between 1978–79 and 1981–82 it decreased by 7.7 percent per year. Sharp increases in student fees generated somewhat more stability in the overall budget.

The decade between 1972 and 1982, therefore, was a difficult period of transition during which the university moved from a gener-ous level of state funding to a level insufficient by itself to support a university of distinction. Given our assessment of future state sup-port and our continuing commitment to quality, we knew that we would have to make difficult adjustments in our program as well as develop new sources of funding.

In the context of our particular situation, we adopted three separate action plans. The first consisted of a careful internal reallo-cation designed to move existing resources to areas of greatest merit and/or promise. The adjustments we made directly affected the di-versity and spectrum of our programs and the source of our funding. We decided that, in order to take our commitment to quality seri-ously, we would have to engage in fewer activities.

In light of these goals, we drew up a Five Year Plan, which would cut approximately $20 million from our General Fund budget (reducing instructional units by 7.3 percent of their base budgets and noninstructional units by 17.1 percent) and reallocate those dollars to our highest priority needs. Our plan called for $16 million in "variable shared" reductions of under 10 to 15 percent, which would apply to all units. The remaining $4 million would be generated by reducing selected program budgets more than 10 to 15 percent; exact reductions were determined by centrally directed program reviews, principally targeting our schools of Art, Education, and Natural Re-sources. Most of these savings were to be realized through cutbacks in staff, primarily in the nonacademic categories. During the first two years of the Five Year Plan, two-thirds of the funds available for reallocation went to improve salaries. The other one-third was assigned to other high-priority needs, such as a graduate student merit scholarship program ($1 million), instructional equipment ($1 million), library, book, and journal acquisitions ($500,000), and new program development ($500,000).

A second plan of action involved renewed efforts to strengthen the partnership between the state of Michigan and the university. In the interest of preserving our vital contribution to the economic and social well-being of the state, we hoped to restore some of the public support that the university had traditionally enjoyed. Initial efforts in this area focused on developing nontraditional support—for example, through new, broad-based, nonprofit entities whose operation would benefit our academic programs.

Our third plan consisted of a greatly enhanced program of private donations that, as with the great private universities, would provide the essential margin of support necessary to build and sustain high quality programs. In 1981–82 the university received a record-breaking $45,570,000 in private support from individuals, corporations, foundations, associations, and other sources, placing us twelfth among all colleges and universities, public or private. Moreover, between 1978–79 and 1981–82, the percentage of alumni supporting the university rose from 25.4 to 37.3 percent, well above the national average for public (13.6 percent) and private (24.3 percent) institutions. The major component of our program for private giving, however, was the Campaign for Michigan, a university-wide, five-year project launched in 1983. Its goal was to raise $80 million for much-needed facilities and another $80 million in endowment for faculty support and student financial aid.

Together these efforts, based on disciplined self-help, restored state appropriations, and enhanced private support, constituted an integrated program to preserve and enhance the mission and performance of the university.

Conclusions

Studies of the dynamics of group organization suggest that two elements must remain in tension to permit change over time: security and challenge. Too little security will cause a paralyzing level of anxiety, while too little challenge may result in isolation from new ideas and practices. While it may be easier to continue expanding, universities faced by a more restrictive environment and a more painful process of adjustment can also become stronger, if they act wisely.

Declining support from the federal government, for example, will require some of the following adjustments: (1) increased tuition (transferring the burden of adjustment to students); (2) increased support from other sources (e.g., states, foundations, individuals); (3) decreased research and/or education activities, with a possible redefinition of the boundaries between research universities and other institutions in the United States and abroad; and (4) increased productivity (i.e., more efficiency) in both education and research.

In most cases, all these adjustments—and others—will be made. I believe, however, that the first two are not viable long-run solutions. The first, the "tuition option," has already been invoked often enough to cause regrettable changes in the composition of the student body. As to the second, other "patrons" have their own agendas to consider and may unduly influence the nature of some faculty activities. We must therefore focus on the other categories—increasing productivity, reallocating assets into areas of highest priority, and divesting some activities to other universities, partnerships, or institutions. Only with a historical view of the research university as a continually evolving institution can we undertake the kind of fundamental changes that will best ensure our future.

Furthermore, it is only worth contemplating changes that actually release resources to cover existing or developing shortfalls. Many campus discussions become tautological, simply calling for increased funding and proposing various schemes to secure more of the available federal or corporate research support. Such proposals may be appropriate, but they are as likely to cost money as to generate a surplus to cover existing shortfalls. Often these ideas can make up deficits only by altering the nature of the institution—a process that should receive careful discussion in each case. Since university teaching and research—even sponsored research—are subsidized activities, university administration in one sense consists of allocating subsidies in a manner most likely to achieve the university's overall objectives. In such an environment, adding more activities solves few budget shortfalls except those arising from the burden of fixed costs.

To change effectively, universities may also have to consider altering their management and governance structures in order to achieve their goals. No existing practice should be exempt from reconsideration, whether tenure practices, existing layers of administration, the disciplinary structure of academic units, or incentives to appropriate turnover (or stability) in staff and faculty. We should take as little for granted as possible.

It is difficult to conceive and thus to articulate what will ultimately sustain higher education. Past sacrifices made in our behalf helped to preserve many of the academic communities that we are proud to belong to. Now some of us may in turn be called upon to make sacrifices in order to maintain our institutions as places to which talented faculty, staff, and students will aspire. As Walter Lippmann noted, "Besides the happiness and the security of the individuals of whom a community is at any moment composed, there are also the happiness and security of the individuals of whom generation after generation it will be composed." To think in this way requires that we balance long-term against short-term interests, the welfare of future participants in this community against our own—as some of our predecessors have done for us.

It is not ordained that universities and their faculties be always richly endowed. It is much more critical that society continue to preserve the university's essential freedom to remain a critic of existing scientific and social arrangements. Our future depends even more on freedom preserved than on full funding retained. New knowledge does not always require funds, but it does require freedom to determine the basic priorities of our investigations. If we in the university community are willing to use society's resources carefully and discerningly and to rededicate ourselves to the critical tasks facing us, the future can become an opportunity gained—an opportunity to address fully the issues to which we have the most to contribute. We cannot simply wish away the difficult sections of the road before us, but neither must we allow those difficulties fully to govern our course.

---

1. This figure of 18 percent is somewhat deceptive because medical care delivery (hospital and professional fees) accounted for one-third of the total university budget.

The Future of the Kaleidoscope:
Medical Education and the University

Despite many false starts and frequent detours, the training of new physicians and the understanding and practice of medicine in the United States have been transformed beyond anything that could have been imagined at the turn of the century. We have trained physicians who, more often than not, demonstrate that new scientific insight works together with medicine's traditional values of compassion and hope to ensure ever more competent care. The profession has, by and large, successfully resisted the seductive but erroneous and dangerous dichotomy between medical science and medical practice. Whatever the deficiencies in our system of medical education—and they are legion—those who have participated in the many significant medical achievements are entitled to our deep and lasting gratitude.

The Environment and the Challenge

Today medical science, the medical profession, and health care delivery are all in the process of transformation. While it is impossible to anticipate the full spectrum of influences that will shape the future environment of the medical practitioner, some landmarks seem clearly visible on the horizon. In particular, the delivery of high-quality medical care will continue to be influenced by a rapidly changing base of knowledge and understanding. Moreover, new institutions and modes of practice will increasingly affect our health delivery systems. Thus, existing relationships among various aspects of our health care network will be substantially altered.

In this climate, the principal challenge for medical education is how to ensure that medical practice can respond adequately to new and often unpredictable developments. To meet its responsibilities to society, the profession will need to overcome its natural loyalty to traditions and existing practice patterns and instead eagerly adapt to new procedures and behaviors. In the next decades, the continual reshaping of their role will require physicians routinely to integrate thoughtful inquiry into their professional lives.

We must, then, construct an educational experience and a form of professional life that permanently connect the practitioner to the evolving knowledge base. This project is, of course, fraught with difficulties. Significant changes in practice take time, subject the physician to uncertainty, generate anxiety of all kinds, and will not be accomplished by issuing edicts or news releases or by publishing learned articles. We must confront the genuine challenge of persuading medical professionals to focus on how they *might* practice medicine instead of how they *have.* Their attention must be drawn not only to new medical procedures but to new social organizations for the delivery of health care.

To accomplish this objective, we will need to integrate the world of academic medicine much more thoroughly with the world of practice. At the very least, the system of medical education must better anticipate the needs of medical practice by forming close communication links with those organizations and individuals that must cooperate in order to restructure the practice arena.

The clinical responsibilities of medical school faculty members may enhance their professional development as teachers and scholars, but these duties do not, in themselves, adequately connect or commit the faculty to the world of practice. Our challenge, therefore, is not only to link practitioners to the evolving knowledge base but to better coordinate the scientific agenda with the exigencies of practice and, thus, with the real needs of the profession and society. In other words, the changes we face in medical practice require us to alter not only the system of medical education but the scholarly and research agenda of medical school faculty.

It is critical for the medical scientist to understand that useful technological change depends on professional experience as well as on theoretical knowledge and controlled experiments. In the vast majority of cases, new technologies and procedures require substantial feedback from the field before they are perfected. The underlying science, even if well understood, usually deals with a more limited set of circumstances than those faced by practitioners in the field. Moving from a controlled to a clinical setting introduces new uncertainties, and field results almost always alter the initial protocols developed in the laboratory. Through extensive experience in actual practice, a particular problem is often reframed and its solution thereby modified.

Knowledge is not simply a collection of facts and relationships that we currently believe in. Professional knowledge consists of principles from basic science, solutions to particular problems derived from basic and applied science, a set of attitudes and values, and a method for coping with uncertainty. Accumulated medical knowledge is organized and applied differently to explore immediate solutions to a problem than to develop fundamental comprehension of a particular biological subsystem. It is imperative that medical scientists and medical practitioners recognize these differences and more constructively address one another's concerns.

Our first challenge, therefore, is to better connect the practicing physician to the evolving knowledge base and the scientific agenda to the world of practice. Our second challenge is to construct an educational experience that aids physicians in molding their practice effectively and cooperatively into the kaleidoscope of institutions and relationships that will comprise the future of the medical profession. One aspect of these evolving relationships—that between the university and the medical profession—deserves further consideration.

Medical Education and the University

It is a commonplace that medical science and medical practice have been remarkably transformed since the turn of the century. It is equally well known that during the same period the role of the university in American medical education has been dramatically strengthened. What is often overlooked, however, is the parallel transformation in the nature and role of America's colleges and universities during this time. This metamorphosis was absolutely central to the capacity of universities to play a new and expanded role in medical education—a role that we now take quite for granted. Further, if we are to consider the future of high quality medical education and the role the university is to play in it, we will have to anticipate the evolution of the university as well as the changing characteristics of medical science and medical practice.

Let us first outline the historic relationship between medical education and the university in the United States. In American universities, medical colleges and hospitals initially developed along quite independent paths. Graduate medical education itself unfolded as a hospital-based, not a university-based, activity. In addition, American medical education in the early years depended heavily on foreign institutions: we imported trained physicians and foreign texts, as well as relying on American students to study abroad. The foreign medical graduate was a central figure in early American medicine. In addition, in the three centuries preceding our own, both medical schools and universities were eclipsed by other institutions and practices in the development of health care professionals and new modes of delivery. In this century, of course, the ties among medical education, patient care, and the university have been greatly strengthened but hardly perfected. Indeed, the potential vitality of our system of medical education continues to be sapped by a lack of integration among its major components.

During the same era that medical education was forging links to the university, the university itself was beginning a critical set of changes. Chief among them was its slow transformation from a center of dogma to a center of inquiry. Just as in medical history the stifling authority of Galen and his followers preceded the atmosphere of open inquiry and progress that marks contemporary medicine, so from colonial times until this century, institutions of higher education in America were largely centers of orthodoxy. Only in the twentieth century, with the transfer of power from trustees to faculty and the emergence of academic freedom, did university faculties begin to concentrate on shaping new ideas rather than clinging to authority. The modern research university, committed to both education and scholarship, developed in close parallel with modern medicine. The uniquely American tradition of community-based higher education also had important consequences for the development of modern medical education. This tradition, for example, allowed entire segments of the health care industry to create partnerships with many of the nation's universities. Thus, in our century simultaneous and mutually reinforcing revolutions have transmuted medical science, medical practice, and the American university.

There is nothing inevitable or fixed about the extent and nature of university involvement in medical education. Although medical schools have played a critical role in the history of the medical profession, their importance and their relationship to the university have, through time, undergone a number of modifications. The future of this relationship will depend on evolving conditions in the medical profession and the university, and on the willingness and capacity of all parties to adapt and change.

The Challenge of Progress, Specialization, and Integration

The enormous changes in modern medicine and in the modern university have created some new and unexpected challenges. One challenge that bears critically on the future of medical education is the centrifugal force of academic specialization, which necessitates growing interaction with and dependence on external institutions—both academic and nonacademic. On the one hand, specialization is a source of great strength for our research universities. But it can potentially turn into a source of weakness as well, for at times the centrifugal forces threaten to drive all the separate groups within the university community away from the core and to the periphery.

This tendency conjures up a fearful image of individual disciplines as isolated encampments on the brave new frontier of knowledge. In this condition, they could not effectively meet either their teaching or their scholarly obligations. We would have lost not only the synergy between teaching and research and the capacity to integrate diverse insights into the human condition but also a crucial component of the energy that sustains a modern academic community.

For medical education, the effects of this extreme specialization may be detrimental. Medicine exists at the intricate intersection of the biological, psychosocial, and behavioral sciences, where the physician and the patient are jointly drawing on their life experiences, on medical science, and on medical practice to sustain and improve the quality of life. If the education of future physicians takes place in a university environment removed from this reality by the growing fragmentation of the various departments, the profession may wish to turn elsewhere to train personnel.

Despite these possible consequences, nowhere in the university community have centrifugal forces been more acute than in medicine. They are evident not only in the threatened isolation of the medical school departments from the rest of the university but in the partial and growing isolation of these departments from one another. In many cases, even subspecialties within a given department, such as surgery, are increasingly isolated from one another. In part this development reflects the greatly increased affluence of these units due to substantial, externally funded research programs and the operation of clinical practice plans. It also results from our tendency to divide the human medical condition—and thus the science, the curriculum, and the mode of health care delivery—into seemingly self-contained subsystems. Despite the necessity and benefits of specialization, these developments have worked, in many cases, to undermine the academic leadership of medical schools as a whole and to unnecessarily fragment both patient care and educational programs.

Increased specialization in a science like physics will eventually lead (via supersymmetry or other theories) to a greater simplicity and a greater comprehension of the ultimate constituents of matter as well as the origin and dynamic evolution of our universe. In medicine, however, the individual is the ultimate unit of concern. As medical science becomes increasingly specialized, it becomes easier to lose sight of this simple and obvious point. Needless to say, faculties, department chairs, deans, and university administrations must also be held to account for failing to sustain a more appropriate vision.

One irony of the present situation is that—as basic research has moved to the molecular level and research results can be quickly transformed into clinical applications—the scientific agenda should now be drawing many medical departments closer together. The academic disciplines, however, have not responded speedily to these developments, particularly in their teaching programs. The result is a new and growing gap between the teaching and research programs of many units. For the moment, then, existing departmental structures and loyalties may be preventing the most creative combinations of efforts in the training of future physicians and the treatment of patients.

These centrifugal forces and the resulting tendency toward isolation of disciplines and teaching programs pose a threat not only to the future quality of medical education but to the capacity of universities to continue their key role in the education of future practitioners. It may, therefore, be time to consider breaking down the existing hierarchy of relationships by restructuring both certain medical school departments and the relationship between university-based medical schools and the world of practice, including specialty boards and residency review committees.

Medical students are introduced to the practice of medicine as soon as their clinical experiences begin. But these experiences consist of a poorly orchestrated mixture of university, certifying board, and review committee demands—all symbolized by the mixture of university faculty and residents they encounter as instructors. Typically, the residents are department-based in their loyalties, are not members of the governing faculty, and are not consulted on the overall structure of the educational program within which they are major actors. Like the residents, the faculty owe their primary allegiance to individual departments, which often do not rank the integrated overall training of future physicians as their first priority. The centrifugal forces of specialization are thus amplified by the centrifugal forces of the institutional arrangements that characterize clinical practice and education in the teaching hospital setting.

Unfortunately, these forces cannot be indefinitely contained within the boundaries of university life as we know it. The potential contribution of this nation's universities to medical science, medical education, and the medical profession would be seriously undermined by the further isolation of medical school departments and their research efforts from one another and from the rest of the university.

How important is university association for the long-run health of medical education? I would argue that it is vital. Medicine is a science, a vocation, and a profession, which means that medical education must apply science to a particular human purpose. In a world of rapidly evolving knowledge, the entire profession must be able to move continuously outside existing assumptions and practices, whether they be institutional arrangements, medical practices and procedures, or our accumulated knowledge base. It is apparent that a vibrant science requires a constant struggle with current ideas and understandings. In the next decades, however, a vibrant profession, especially one dependent on new trends in science, must also struggle constantly with existing social structures and practice patterns. Only in this way can the medical profession expect society to continue recognizing its claim to special competence.

All professions make claims to special rights and privileges, but society grants them only to those groups that continue to demonstrate both their technical and moral capacity to serve society's needs. The challenge for medical education, therefore, is to locate itself in an environment that has the best chance of nourishing new ideas and educating physicians to respond thoughtfully to innovations.

If medical scientists become isolated from the broader scientific community by closing themselves off in special institutes—either within or outside the academic community—they will fail in their ultimate objectives. It is the dual relationship of medicine to the scientific world and the medical profession that makes the modern university potentially such a strategically useful place to locate important segments of both medical science and medical education. If, however, the university community should lose its own coherence and become a colony of isolated efforts, it would cease to be able to play its current role for medicine, for other professions, or for the broader world of scholarship. Only thoughtful, vigilant concern for the university as an academic community can ensure our ability to meet our responsibilities in teaching and scholarship in the years ahead.

As we consider ways to enhance the future quality of medical education, therefore, we must direct some of our attention to the core of university life and the core of medical school educational programs. In both cases, we must revitalize and reinforce the fabric that weaves the diverse elements of our academic community together. Only if we reestablish the coherent academic leadership of the university as a whole can the research university remain an institution capable of fully supporting the needs of medicine. Similarly, only by reestablishing the coherence of medical school programs themselves and the lifelong education of practitioners can our programs in medical education meet their responsibilities.

A New Relationship: An Opportunity for Leadership

If the university and the medical profession are to continue their productive relationship, however, a new and modified association between academia and the profession must be considered. Change will be required within all components of the current system, but I will address only two areas.

First, in order for medical education to remain part of the modern university, it must be directly involved in the following tasks: (a) developing in its students the skills and values of professional practice, (b) initiating productive dialogue among faculty, students, and the broad world of practice, and (c) becoming an agent for change in both medical science and medical practice. All this can be accomplished only if all participants not only learn a set of skills but also appreciate the broader social purpose they serve.

We need not worry so much about the baccalaureate education of future physicians. The real challenges lie in the integration of the M.D. curriculum, the residency years, and the learning environment of the practicing physician. Undergraduate preparation in such areas as ethics or decision making under uncertainty will have little or no impact on the practice of medicine unless and until these issues become an integral part of medical training as well.

Second, I wish to propose some possible new relationships between university-based medical schools and the sphere of medical practice. My first proposal is that university programs play a more central (not necessarily dominant) role in the residency years and in the continuing education of physicians. For example, academic and clinical requirements of residency programs and the certification of residents could be a joint activity of the medical school faculty, the specialty boards, the residency review committees, and/or the representatives of practicing physicians. In such an arrangement, the medical school—not just its individual departments—should be represented. Whatever the system, we must better ensure that the residency is a genuine educational experience and not just an apprenticeship program. This is critical to the quality of professional life.

A second proposal is that practitioners participate meaningfully in the M.D. training experience. Why have we not been more successful in integrating practicing physicians into the clinical instruction program both as teachers and as students? One way to achieve this would be for the national residency review committees and specialty boards to have additional representation in the programs of our medical schools. Such suggestions will, of course, be considered controversial—even dangerous—on many university campuses, where issues of quality and independence will be raised immediately. But I still believe that the monopoly of medical school faculty on the M.D. curriculum may not be the best possible arrangement for the challenges of the next decades. Alternatives ought to be carefully evaluated. The recent effort of the American Board of Internal Medicine to promote "humanism" in the training process affords an excellent example of how specialty boards can appropriately influence curricula.

Third, the post-residency learning environment of practicing physicians must be dramatically upgraded, but in a manner that demonstrates our support and respect for the work they are doing. It is critical to remember that the practicing physician represents a valuable resource for the medical scientist as well as a lifelong student. In any case, we can no longer allow large numbers of physicians to drift into incompetence.

Many issues remain to be worked out, and these suggestions may well be replaced by far superior ideas. Whatever the ultimate shape of the plan, however, we must strive for a new partnership that better integrates the disparate segments of our current medical education system. A knowledge-based profession now requires an educational experience that coordinates knowledge production, knowledge acquisition, experience, and application. The educational system we devise must also retain its vitality and relevance for the professional's entire career, thus facilitating the process of self-renewal.

What is absolutely certain is that the current environment provides unusually fertile ground for imaginative and courageous leadership. We feel buffeted by external circumstances in part because various vested interests have prevented much of organized medicine—including academic health centers—from adequately responding to changing circumstances. When medicine itself failed to take full advantage of new knowledge in order, for example, to decrease length of stay and/or increase the use of more convenient and efficient outpatient procedures, society found other social mechanisms to accomplish this objective. In the process, the profession abdicated some of its leadership and, thus, may have forfeited some of its rights and privileges. If the university and the profession do not seize this moment to strengthen each other and exert capable leadership, the future will belong to someone else.

Finally, I turn from the world of medicine to the world of art for images of medicine and medical education. Great paintings by Rembrandt, Feyen-Perrin, Eakins, and Rivera may help us foresee a portrait of the profession to be painted in the year 2000.

Rembrandt's famous portrait of the Dutch physician Dr. Ephraim Bueno still powerfully conveys the public's image of the quintessential physician—wise, thoughtful, knowledgeable, gentle, and humane. Yet nothing in this canvas suggests the role of industry or of science and scientific understanding, which played no part in seventeenth-century medicine. Juxtaposing two paintings of an anatomy lesson—one from the seventeenth century, the other from the nineteenth—indicates that medical practice had progressed little in the intervening years. In Rembrandt's depiction of Dr. Tulp's anatomy lesson, virtually all the participants seem to be drawing away from the cadaver, perhaps in fear or in awe of a greater power at work. The nineteenth-century French painting of Dr. Velpeau's anatomy lesson by Auguste Feyen-Perrin displays very much the same attitude, with the "magic" in the doctor's uplifted hands dominating the scene. A few hundred years had passed, but little new understanding of biology had penetrated the physician's clinic. In Thomas Eakins's famous portrait of Dr. Gross in the Gross Clinic (1875), the general composition remains unchanged from the Rembrandt or the Feyen-Perrin picture, but the spirit is entirely different. Here we see the emerging influence of scientific understanding and the possibility of effective human intervention in the relationship of Dr. Gross to both his subject and his students. The "magic" has been replaced by new knowledge and insight.

A more contemporary series of images is taken from the great murals of Diego Rivera in the Detroit Institute of Arts. Painted in the 1930s, this remarkable series forcefully evokes the new role of medical science and the health industry. For the first time, we see a separation of medical science and medical practice, with the physician as a laboratory scientist who is somewhat removed from the broad human purpose that should always inform the profession. The doctors themselves are portrayed as dedicated, but forbidding, cold, and isolated—quite different from Rembrandt's Dr. Bueno. Rivera was, of course, contrasting the constructive and destructive results of science. A great deal of progress has been made since he painted his murals. Many of his fears have proved unfounded, but aspects of his vision remain as challenges to us today. We must work to ensure that the painting of the physician in the year 2000 reunites all aspects of the medical kaleidoscope in a manner that most enhances the human condition.

Values in
Higher Education

The National Debate on
Higher Education

During the last decade the American public has been anxiously following an ongoing debate over the nature and quality of education in our nation's schools and, more recently, in our colleges and universities. In October, 1986, on the occasion of Harvard College's 350th anniversary, the Secretary of Education, William J. Bennett, once again joined the fray by broadly criticizing the current state of American higher education. As in the past, the secretary charges that the higher education community pursues its share of the nation's resources more vigorously than it does the education and moral development of its students. Specifically, Secretary Bennett charges that:

A. Higher education is not efficient. That is, it is less than fully responsible in its use of the nation's resources.
B. Higher education plays an inadequate role in the moral well-being of its students and in the wholehearted reinforcement of the chief values that inform American life and Western civilization in general.

In addition, the secretary calls for a restructuring of federal financial aid policies to place a greater burden on students (or their families) who choose to attend high-priced institutions. It is useful to recall that Secretary Bennett had initially suggested a more general curtailment of student financial aid, depicting contemporary college students as spoilt rich kids with enough money for expensive beach holidays and stereo systems. When this perspective appeared unpopular, he shifted the focus of his criticism from the students to their teachers.

With respect to efficiency and resource use, there is a sense in which the secretary's point is well taken. When speaking from public platforms, the faculty and administration of our nation's colleges and universities often articulate their resource requirements more fully than their educational agenda. In addition, the rhetoric of the higher education community sometimes exhibits a pious and self-congratulatory tone and often betrays an attitude that widespread support is a kind of natural right that does not need to be earned. We cannot simply state that ignorance is more expensive than education; we must demonstrate that our stewardship of the nation's resources is executed as well as possible. Americans have begun to notice that the price for higher education services is rising faster than the general price level, and they are questioning the lack of apparent productivity gains.

The actual efficiency of higher education, however, is hard to assess. Education is a service, and economists have had problems developing adequate measures of productivity in such industries. In addition, rapid qualitative changes in the activity under study make it difficult to measure the rate of change in productivity. We can, however, claim that, as long as there is competition for faculty and students, higher education will remain considerably more competitive than many industries, even though universities are nonprofit organizations. At the same time, state universities, for example, have a certain monopolistic power in that resident students can "shop" among universities in their own state, but not among other states, if they wish to avail themselves of the state subsidy. Some private universities can be similarly monopolistic because of their actual or perceived "special" qualities, which work to their advantage even when groundless. In any case, the secretary may be right about the inefficiency of higher education, and, regardless, we ought to be more vigilant in searching out methods to improve its productivity.

In my own public role, I have often pleaded for additional support for higher education, but at the same time I have acknowledged that higher education should contribute its fair share of any resource conservation necessary to the national interest. In fact, it is still genuinely unclear whether our national interest requires an increase or a decrease in our level of resource commitment to higher education. We and the secretary ought to be addressing this important issue directly. Rhetoric and confrontation are no substitute for communication and change.

The secretary also calls for greater emphasis within university curricula on the moral development of students and on the values that should inform our society. Perhaps he is responding to the undoubted deterioration of our level of commitment to common values and shared objectives. In this era of transition our whole culture quite naturally feels expelled from a common community of memory without having yet fully developed a new vision on which to focus our common aspiration.

Once again, Secretary Bennett raises important issues, reminding us that not all values have equal standing in our society. There is, for us, more than a difference of opinion between vegetarianism and cannibalism. Even a free and pluralistic society has some absolute values (e.g., honesty, kindness, respect for law, responsibility), but we have not yet completely met the difficult challenge of examining and articulating them in full. So it may be true that colleges and universities are not paying enough attention to this critical area of our national life. However, Secretary Bennett's request also presents those of us in higher education with a few dilemmas.

First, the secretary gives no indication of how we might approach this task without establishing a moral orthodoxy that would fundamentally undermine the nature of our academic community. Indeed, it is even possible to infer a particular orthodoxy from the very tone of Secretary Bennett's remarks. It is extraordinarily difficult to agree on which values, precisely, we are supposed to teach because values are not discovered by reason but simply adopted. Indeed, war can be explained as one of the few available means, however irrational, to assert the primacy of a particular view. I firmly believe that higher education should not endorse a "complete" set of values but should rather, through its educational programs, ensure that students and faculty fully comprehend the underlying vision of our country and our civilization, keep the fundamental problems of our humanity and our society before us, and continue to search for new alternatives. Students will not readily gain such an experience elsewhere in our society, and it is more important than being useful and/or popular.

Second, the secretary's reported comments ignore the social context within which we all operate and which deeply affects not only the morality of our own actions but our potential to infuse our students with a greater concern for the moral implications of their education. Moral training in the helping professions, for instance, can only occur in the context of our nation's present social policies. Currently, our country has decreased its efforts to assist in the nutritional, emotional, and cognitive development of young children; a rising proportion of our students enter grade school with significant cognitive deficits; and increasing numbers of families must send their children to schools where they will be exposed to illicit drugs and perhaps even shootings. I applaud Secretary Bennett's call for higher education to examine its role in instilling the values that make it possible for a free, pluralistic society to prosper. This moral education will, however, remain incomplete until people like the secretary step forward and help us address some of the environmental issues within which we and the students we train must work.

Nevertheless, Secretary Bennett has raised an interesting, if challenging, problem, and higher education probably has not responded as thoughtfully as it should. In my view, neither our curriculum nor our scholarship adequately addresses these issues. Few of us understand the difference between mastery of what is true (the natural world) and the mystery of what is good and beautiful but not now accessible as truth (the "supernatural"). Academia may be free of external prejudices, but it has an abundance of internal prejudices. Perhaps, as a first step, we should begin taking stronger measures to safeguard a fundamental value of academic communities—the value of openness and the free exchange of ideas. We all know that intolerance of various kinds continues to plague many colleges and universities; some ideas never reach an open forum on the nation's campuses.

The great treasure of the university is that its knowledge base and critical capacity do not serve civil, church, or other authorities. We have an obligation, therefore, to counteract the convention and prejudice that always abound in society. A great characteristic of Western liberal democracies is that the central government has largely given over control of the economic sector to private enterprise and the production of new knowledge to universities. We must continue to believe in this mission of universities and actively pursue it. Commitment, a common set of binding values, and a passion driven by a certain moral excitement are required to sustain important institutions. Good sense and intelligence are not enough. We academics have to come to care as people about the scholarly issues before us—whether in art, religion, philosophy, social criticism, or biology—rather than just analyzing them. Commitment is critical. Without anguish we cannot pass on a worthwhile legacy to the next generation. We must be aware of the extraordinary difficulty of the choices before us.

To accomplish this, higher education must be a dialogue, not just a monologue. The best learning takes place in an atmosphere where students are actively involved, where the institution has high expectations of them, and where they receive adequate assessment and feedback. Creating such an atmosphere is a great challenge. Unhappily, we excel at "private" research more than at public discourse—that is, at teaching one another. We often forget that education consists not only of comprehension and reasoning but of transformation and reflection. Moreover, Secretary Bennett seems to want us to focus this crucial activity within the academic community—especially on students and their development—and spend less time advising others in our society what *they* should do. He does not like what academics have been saying.

With respect to federal financial aid, Bennett offers an intriguing proposal. Essentially, he argues that the level of aid should not depend on the price of a particular education, which—like a "cost plus" contract—encourages inefficiencies. Instead, he proposes that students receive a flat amount of aid. Such an arrangement would, of course, substantially benefit low-tuition institutions and hurt higher-tuition schools. It is important to understand that low-tuition institutions are not necessarily either low cost or efficient. They could, for instance, simply be low quality. We would not want federal policy to encourage the proliferation of such institutions. In any case, Bennett's proposition raises a number of serious questions, such as: (1) Should our society prefer and reward state subsidies as a substitute for federal subsidies of education? (2) Do we care if Harvard is available only to the rich? (3) Will such a scheme encourage efficiency, and, if so, how? (4) What impact will such a policy have on the plurality of approaches that characterize American higher education?

These critical questions have not been fully addressed by the higher educational community. Unfortunately, Secretary Bennett's stance has been so confrontational and higher education so defensive that it is easy to lose sight of the real issues. Such questions, however, are sure to form the center of continuous controversy in the years ahead.

Secretary Bennett's comments follow on the heels of other assessments, such as *Involvement in Learning: Reading the Potential of Higher Education* (1984), *To Reclaim a Legacy* (1984), and *Integrity in the College Curriculum* (1985), all focused on both the real and imagined problems of higher education in the United States. There are many reasons for this recent preoccupation with higher education. One is the increasingly popular notion that our nation's leadership in economic, political, military, and cultural affairs depends on our achievements in science and technology and, therefore, in education. Seldom in our history has higher education been the locus of so many of our national aspirations. A second reason for our concern is that we are reevaluating the role of the federal government and, in particular, the nature of the federal responsibility, if any, for the health of our educational system. A third is that we are troubled by the uneven capacity of our system of higher education to respond effectively to significant social change, such as the increased participation of women and minorities in the work force or the social disintegration that marks some of our nation's communities.

These diverse factors have engendered a number of contradictory themes in our national discussion of higher education. On the one hand, we regularly celebrate the achievements of American higher education and its potential for helping our nation attain a new level of leadership in the world community. On the other hand, as these reports testify, there is a widespread conviction that many of our aspirations remain unfulfilled, even that higher education is not simply failing to meet its full potential but quietly slipping into decay.

In addition to these well-meaning but critical reports, a number of other recent events and controversies have tarnished the public image of higher education. Athletic scandals, for example, seem to some observers to reveal a certain hypocrisy in the self-righteous professions of many university presidents. These suspicions are reinforced by the public perception that the few reports of research fraud are but the tip of the proverbial iceberg; that universities are protecting their own and only outside regulators can restore integrity to these autonomous institutions. In addition, there is a growing cynicism about what is viewed as the self-serving nature of the peer review system and the associated notion that quality is nothing but a device to protect insiders and exclude outsiders (*New York Times*, September 29, 1986).

Finally, some critics point to reimbursement for the indirect costs of externally sponsored research as a fraudulent diversion of funds—this despite the fact that indirect costs are perfectly acceptable for all other government contractors and within all other sectors of our economy, and that universities have by far the lowest indirect costs of all government contractors. This disturbing cynicism, often supported by university faculties, is, I believe, a symptom of a certain underlying ambivalence about continued public support for higher education. Inside the university community itself, it may be a symptom of a sharply decreased faculty commitment to the individual university campus as a coherent academic community.

This pervasive uneasiness, together with the crushing indictment of higher education in these national reports, makes it mandatory for university faculties and administrators to fashion some response. It is in our interest to shake off our complacency about continued public support, honestly appraise our own achievements and commitments in view of the issues raised, and participate actively in the debate. We cannot afford simply to dismiss these concerns, most of which are well intended, and risk the accusation that we are putting our vested interests ahead of reforms that might better serve the country's long-term needs. Unfortunately, there may be a growing mismatch between what we in higher education perceive and what the public at large believes to be our contemporary contribution to society.

As a first step toward such a response, let us evaluate the recent reports on higher education. Their common themes are simple to summarize. Without adducing any supporting evidence, they charge that undergraduate education has undesirably narrowed and grown increasingly vocational in its emphasis. This problem is often expressed as the abandonment of the traditional liberal arts curriculum. The reports also charge college faculties with abdicating their responsibilities for undergraduate education as a whole. Faculties, they claim, have narrowed their focus to the specialized concerns of individual departments, where they deploy a curricular structure and associated review system that effectively prevent their involvement in overall curricular concerns. Further, the reports decry the failure of the nation's colleges and universities to adequately foster the shared values so critical to binding our pluralistic society into a genuine community.

Finally, plucking an old chestnut from the fire, they accuse college and university faculties of abrogating their teaching responsibilities in pursuit of their specialized research interests. The simple fact that, nationally, the overwhelming majority of college faculty members do not engage in significant research activity never seems to diminish the emotion behind this particular accusation. Once again, the public concern apparently reflects an underlying wariness about support for higher education. In this context, research is simply a useful object upon which to project other frustrations with the system.

What are we to make of these charges? Whatever my views on the merits of these particular claims, I share the general sentiment of the reports that improvements in higher education are not only possible but necessary. The current structure of American higher education and the role of the contemporary university in American society have evolved over time in response to a changing world. It would be a special intellectual arrogance to assume that this process of change had reached its zenith and that additional progress was unnecessary or impossible. On the contrary, we can assume that the next decades will witness continuing modifications in any American college or university that wishes to retain its vitality.

Thus, I accept, even welcome, the expressed need for change. But I find serious faults with the present crop of reports on three grounds. First, they treat American higher education as a monolithic structure. By indirection, at least, they attack what surely must be one of the great strengths of our system of higher education—its diversity. American higher education is a vast, decentralized, unplanned enterprise that nevertheless generates—through its diversity, autonomy, and a system of competitive cooperation—an enormously valuable social product. However justified the common call for more order in our national life might be, it would be foolish to advocate greater uniformity and government control in higher education when competition for students, faculty, facilities, and prestige has created a remarkably responsive set of institutions, despite their anarchic structure and the limited capacity of prospective students to discuss quality. Second, the reports are singularly lacking in any data to support their arguments. In fact, they all rely on rhetoric rather than careful study to buttress their proposals for wide-ranging educational reform.

Finally, rather than speak of the undoubted need for thoughtful change, the reports warn of decline. Instead of cautioning us about the dangers of complacency, they raise the rhetoric of disaster. In this respect, I believe their historical perspective to be fundamentally flawed. To justify their inference of decline, these jeremiads would have to draw on both a sound assessment of the state of contemporary higher education *and* an analysis of the history that has brought us to the brink of the present disaster. They do neither. The simple truth is that the reports as a whole are much more concerned with capturing public attention than engaging in an informed debate grounded in the unique historical dynamic of American higher education. The result is a seriously misleading assessment of the current condition of higher education as well as a flawed perspective of its history.

What passes for history in these reports is the myth of a previous Golden Age of higher education, naively located in the antebellum liberal arts colleges. Such a myth neglects the transformative events of our own century: the momentous shifts in both the pace of discovery and the role of new knowledge as well as the more strategic place that American higher education has assumed in our national life. Ignoring these particular aspects of American higher education renders any subsequent analysis suspect.

The reports do raise legitimate and appropriate concerns regarding curricular coherence, literacy, and historical understanding, but these concerns are far overshadowed by half-informed rhetoric about an ailing monolith of academic decay, crisis, and neglect. We should not for a moment doubt the necessity of rational change or the dangers of complacency. In this respect, however, the analyses contained in these reports and their suggested directions are not very helpful. Whether or not they will inspire thoughtful deliberation remains to be seen. So far they have done considerable mischief, and it is now up to us, on the basis of the actual achievements of higher education, to correct the course of the debate. In so doing we must remain open to change and willing to admit to our shortcomings.

Openness in an Academic Community

Most contemporary university communities strive to be open societies in which faculties and students freely share the results of their research as well as discussing alternative or evolving ideas. This openness of heart and mind is an essential ingredient of university research and teaching programs and a prerequisite of our intellectual credibility. Indeed, the primary role of the university should perhaps be to foster an environment of intellectually disciplined free inquiry and exchange of ideas. In this environment, each faculty member and student must act as trustee for the value of intellectual openness and the unimpeded exchange of ideas, disciplined only by that careful scrutiny necessary to ensure honesty, completeness, and the use of appropriately rigorous analysis. In such a setting, all new scientific findings belong, in some sense, to the community.

This may be an idealized version of a university community, but it is a vision toward which many of us aspire, as the following quotation from a Stanford faculty resolution testifies: "The university operates in and wishes to preserve an environment of free and open intellectual inquiry. Such an environment is valued as an end in itself and is demonstrably most effective in generating additions to knowledge . . . while simultaneously enhancing freedom in our society." One strong incentive toward this kind of openness is the desirability and necessity of working relationships between scholars and advanced students and, in particular, the obligation to promote the interests of graduate students. The intimate linkage between scholarly research and advanced training, in my opinion, both requires and produces a certain candor in the exchange of ideas.

No academic community, of course, has ever been completely open. Individual students and scholars have, for various reasons, evolved some of their ideas in private. Most scholars have not felt obliged to reveal all their thoughts—on demand—to any arbitrary member of the academic community. On the contrary, many of us have considered it a prerogative to develop an idea or discovery within a restricted circle of colleagues, at least temporarily, before sharing it with the broader community of scholars. The freedom to publish has never been construed as the obligation to publish before emerging ideas can be carefully and critically evaluated. The many motives for such delays and restrictions range from legitimate concerns for quality to more questionable tactics of self-aggrandizement.

Another limit on the atmosphere of openness and intellectual sharing in American universities has traditionally been the notion of "intellectual property," which allows individual members of the academic community to profit financially from their efforts at the university. For example, universities as institutions normally disdain all financial rights to copyrightable material. Attitudes toward patentable material, while often quite different, usually also permit individual financial gain.

To some degree, then, we have always had to compromise the academic values of openness and independence in order to meet other needs and duties. In addition, American universities have, from the very beginning, had to balance their responsibilities to the world of scholarship against their responsibilities to the communities that supported them. Academics have a long tradition of involvement in contemporary issues—ranging from public policy to the private marketplace—some of which create tensions between openness and other academic values. In fact, the three contemporary trends discussed below raise questions about the extent to which the modern research university can and should continue to adhere to the value of academic openness.

Taking Stands on Moral Issues

Universities are currently being exhorted by various interest groups to take official positions on issues such as military research and the U.S. corporate presence in South Africa. Often the groups making such demands are perplexed by the resistance they meet, since they believe their particular perspective promotes the long-term best interest of the human community and, therefore, the university community as well.

The work of the academic community is undeniably related to and supported by a particular set of values, including the value of knowledge, the benefit of fair and open inquiry, respect for other points of view, and the possibility of human progress. In addition, most universities have by now taken a stand on some moral issues, such as affirmative action and human subject research. We must, however, be extremely cautious about adding to this list. Without a means of distinguishing ideas from ideologies, we may undermine the environment that supports our principal commitments and responsibilities. Returning to an earlier model of moral, political, and scientific orthodoxy would undercut academic freedom and open discourse, transforming the character of higher education and impairing the university's capacity to serve society.

It seems ironic that so many different segments of the political spectrum, including both the defense and the antidefense establishments, now want to constrain academic freedom and openness. I believe that both moral objections to war and moral arguments for strong defense too easily become restrictions on our developing knowledge base. Moreover, there are complex questions that require answers before we can take informed positions on these issues. For instance, if we are to limit so-called military research, how do we distinguish it from nonmilitary research when our defense program uses all aspects of modern technology, from the wheel to the laser, as well as our improved understanding of human history and varying cultures? Similarly, can we actually predict the military impact of any particular new piece of knowledge? Will any given new technology, military or otherwise, make nuclear disarmament more or less likely or feasible?

Although academic freedom is not the only value that should inform our actions, we should carefully scrutinize the reasons for every proposed erosion of it. As we prepare to discuss each such proposal, we might ask ourselves these questions:

1. What is the source of the university's right to free inquiry and what is its relation to the society that grants that right? In particular, what obligations accrue from this right?
2. If the university as an institution takes a moral or political stand, what implication does this have for members of the community with other points of view?
3. How do we identify those moral and political issues on which a university should adopt a particular point of view?

For example, is the range of admissible inquiry a matter for administrative decision? If so, under what circumstances do we allow restrictions on teaching and research programs that offend an individual's moral or political values?

To transform moral sentiments into policy statements, we need carefully articulated ideas of the mission of a university and the impact of teaching and research on that mission. I believe that a university remains a creative part of society only as long as it remains an intellectually open community and not the ally of a particular point of view.

Keeping National Security Secrets

The second trend affecting academic openness arises from the vexed relationship between national security and university-based research efforts. In the spring of 1982 many national security advisors were contending that the openness of university research endangers our national security by providing our adversaries easy and open access to the best U.S. science and technology. They argued that such information, flowing freely through the open scientific literature, imperiled both our military and our economic advantage. They proposed to solve this problem by drawing a curtain of secrecy around a broad range of university-based research and educational exchange programs.

In response to these proposals, the National Academy of Sciences established a special Panel on Scientific Communication and National Security, on which I served. This group concluded that, although there was a substantial unwanted flow of U.S. technology to our adversaries, open scientific literature contributed little to it of military significance. In these circumstances, it hardly seemed advisable to threaten the vigor of U.S. science by imposing a cloak of secrecy on important segments of university-based research.

In general, observers interested not only in the progress of U.S. science but in the overall vitality of our national life have long defended the openness and free flow of information that characterize our society. Indeed, the fundamental viability of a democracy depends on maintaining a well-informed electorate with ready access to currently salient ideas and information. Historically, such access has been considered so essential that a strong legal and constitutional framework exists to ensure its continuation.

In addition, the majority of scientists believe that scientific research—particularly basic research—prospers most when the effort is dispersed, even somewhat redundant, but both interdependent and cumulative. Openness and the free flow of information within the scientific community are crucial aspects of such an environment. Restricting the flow of information, scientists argue, limits feedback, postpones the discovery of errors, prevents critical evaluation of scientific efforts, and promotes duplication of efforts. Indeed, our current technological leadership owes its health and vitality to effective communication among scientists and engineers.

Potential national security benefits from restricting the flow of information must also be balanced against potential costs to the nation's fundamental scientific effort. Since scientific expertise is now widely distributed around the globe, our openness assists both colleagues and adversaries abroad, but our own efforts are also increasingly nourished by ideas from foreign scientists. The extra short-term security achieved by restricting the flow of information comes at a price. It affects our efforts in basic research and our efficiency in the transfer of the latest scientific and technological information in both the defense and nondefense areas. In short, security by achievement is better than security by secrecy. Nevertheless, the increasing dependence of the military on a broad spectrum of contemporary developments in science and technology creates an inevitable relationship between current university-based scholarship and national security concerns. Moreover, this relationship is not confined to the areas of physical science and technology but applies to a wide cross-section of university scholarship.

Participating in Commercial Ventures

A third contemporary trend that raises the issue of openness in the academic community is the purportedly increasing involvement of university faculties in research sponsored by private corporations and, in some cases, in direct entrepreneurial activity.[1] Such arrangements can pose difficulties unless they are structured so as to support academic values and objectives. Conflicts of interest and commitment must also be confronted honestly. If properly constructed, monitored, and evaluated, however, working relationships between universities and external agencies can prove mutually beneficial despite their inevitably differing agendas. Through resource and information transfers, these relationships can help improve the quality of particular instructional and research programs, as well as disseminating socially useful knowledge throughout society.

Interestingly, corporate sponsorship of university research usually arises in response to university-based initiatives, often growing out of particular consulting arrangements. University-industrial partnerships have long supplemented the university's central mission by providing valuable research and educational opportunities for students and faculty members, as well as contributing to various industrial efforts. In this sense, universities and corporations recognize a certain community of interest in research and development.

Of course, research activities that cannot be widely shared with colleagues and students or that draw substantial faculty attention away from important educational and research programs can change the nature and quality of the university. In this respect, however, I believe that the long-term academic interests of the university, as well as the economic interests of both the university and industry, actually coincide. In my opinion, sacrificing educational goals or scientific integrity and independence for short-term financial support will, in the long run, adversely affect a university's economic outlook and will deprive industry of what it most needs— trained personnel and an independent source of scientific thinking.

An associated set of issues concerns faculty, students, or staff engaging in direct entrepreneurial activity or taking on substantial management responsibility in an external agency. Such practices can lead to conflicts of commitment and/or interest if those involved can no longer make appropriate decisions on behalf of the university or meet academic responsibilities. For these reasons, faculty members, students, and staff should normally remain primarily committed to the university. As in most matters, however, a balanced and flexible policy, not an overly legalistic one, is desirable. Some type of conflict always arises when a faculty member pursues outside work, but in certain cases it can greatly benefit the university, society, and the individual. Moreover—except for substantial equity interests in outside companies, which are more difficult to resolve—many if not most such conflicts can be largely remedied by disclosure.

Thus, although the contemporary American university primarily seeks to pursue and disseminate learning for its own sake, as well as helping to transmit enduring values, it also engages in the transfer of socially useful knowledge to the marketplace and to society at large. This knowledge transfer is, in many fields, intimately linked to our central educational and research programs. If we decide to perpetuate this function of universities, we will continue to face new and often unexpected questions about the role of openness in our universities and the role of universities in our society.

Structuring Partnerships with External Agencies

Divided commitments are not new to academics, but certain trends in our society demand renewed attention to them: (1) The increasing importance of science (including social science) and technology, not only in the private marketplace but as an instrument of national policy, emphasizes the centrality of American research universities to the overall national effort in basic and applied research. (2) The decreasing time lag between developments in basic research and their profitable commercial application (that is, converting ideas into property), as well as their operational relevance to national security concerns, draws faculty and students closer to a range of national issues—some quite tangential to basic university priorities. (3) The fading line between basic and applied research as well as the rapid transformation of all kinds of research into valuable property creates many new incentives in the university community, some of which may conflict with traditional academic values. (4) The entire process from basic research to product development, sales, and service is now so integrated as to require the ongoing involvement of researchers in all aspects of the process.

These forces are creating a growing interdependence between the American university and the society around it. So we are right to be apprehensive about our capacity to maintain the distinctive role of the university as a haven for the disinterested pursuit of knowledge and criticism of societal arrangements. We must ask whether it is possible to structure partnerships between universities and external agencies—whether corporations, foundations, or government bodies—that advance the separate but overlapping interests of all parties without attenuating the fundamental academic values of openness, scientific integrity, credibility, and independence.

To complicate matters further, we must recognize that large American research universities are confederations of diverse groups. Our colleagues in, for example, music, engineering, philosophy, and medicine not only have differing commitments as scholars and professionals, but also harbor varying visions of the educational process, the nature of creative scholarly activity, the relationship of research to teaching, and their association with the society around them. This diversity of tradition and outlook represents a strength of the university; any policy we implement should respect this pluralism, even as we work to strengthen the shared values and commitments that draw us together as a community.

In my view, these trends require us carefully to consider and articulate what principles should define the nature and extent of relationships between the contemporary university and external agencies. In so doing, we must ensure that these relationships meet societal needs while preserving the fundamental values of the university community. We must, of course, protect our teaching programs, our intellectual independence, our scientific credibility, our capacity for advanced training, and our role as critics of existing arrangements in science and society. But we should try to do so in a way that allows us to maximize our contributions to society and, where possible, to strengthen other essential social and economic institutions. Our environment is changing, and we should respond by both encouraging creative new ideas and renewing our commitment to the most enduring of our academic values.

We might consider some of the following principles for governing our relationships with external agencies.

1. The activity should grow out of, and contribute to, our educational and/or research programs.
2. All agreements should be public and all foreseeable conflicts settled in advance.
3. We should try to guard against the dominance of any single source of funds.
4. In almost all cases the results of the research or education

programs should be open, allowing only for minor delays in the processing of patents or courtesy reviews by sponsors.

5. Arrangements should be structured so that faculty and staff retain a primary long-run commitment to the university. Such a requirement would have implications for the ownership of patents and other related matters.

6. Licensing arrangements should maximize the spread of socially useful knowledge.

7. The flexibility to individualize arrangements, subject to an agreed framework, is highly desirable.

There are, of course, many more issues to be addressed, but I hope these suggestions will stimulate discussion.

Finally, there is the question of whether the university should more fully enter the industrial arena in order to profit from the economic value of campus research development. This could be accomplished, for example, by holding substantial equity interest in enterprises whose products derive from campus-based research. Such a possibility requires careful and, in my opinion, skeptical evaluation. Despite the potential financial advantages, it seems to set up many possible conflicts between a university's financial and academic decisions. This question deserves further discussion and analysis.

We cannot meet our obligations by simply withdrawing to a narrower and narrower spectrum of education and scholarship. Despite our medieval roots, we probably do not wish to reconstruct a monastic cloister, at least not in the whole university. We should also recall that public interest in university scholarship is supported in large part by the hope of eventually useful applications, and there is little freedom without resources. The inevitable tensions between the university as an independent center of new ideas and as a major participant in various national enterprises should be accepted as a natural and even welcome symptom of our complex role in society. We must confront this tension creatively rather than retreating from it.

A certain vigilance, but also a certain flexibility, is essential to the preservation of academic values. There are always forces and tendencies working to compromise our independence, our environment of free and open inquiry, and our integrity as disinterested observers and critics of existing arrangements. Furthermore, corruption is at least latent in all activities. We must assess our current environment honestly and adopt practices that preserve the university's uniqueness while allowing us the fullest appropriate participation in our national life.

1. So far, corporations provide universities with only about 5 percent ($350 million of the $6.5 billion total) of their external research funding.

The Nature, Function, and Future
of Academic Tenure

Most faculty members have devoted little careful thought to the issue of academic tenure, but they are tenaciously attached to it as one of the anchors securing them to the university. Many of them would feel that their membership in the academic community was severely if not irreparably diminished by any substantial modification in the form of academic tenure. They might also greet a university president's speculations on the subject with a great deal of skepticism. After all, tenure was designed in large part to safeguard the academic community and society in general from the ill-considered actions of government officials, trustees, and university administrators. It is with full appreciation for the delicacy of my institutional relationship to tenure that I offer my comments on this vital but emotion-laden issue.

Although not widely understood, even within the academic community, tenure is one of the chief means by which the academic freedom of individual faculty members and, more broadly, of the university itself is protected. Academic freedom, in turn, is thought to be the essential ingredient that enables a modern university to fulfill its function. Without its relationship through academic freedom to the fundamental mission of the modern university, tenure would be merely another personnel policy.

The present moment, when the system of academic tenure is receiving somewhat hostile scrutiny, seems an appropriate time to clarify, redefine, and reinforce our shared notions of this controversial practice. Influential voices, both inside and outside the university, are suggesting that tenure may be inconsistent with the vitality of higher education in the coming decades. These commentators argue that tenure not only works to shield incompetency, create a kind of academic aristocracy, and block the access of women and minorities to university positions, but it also deprives universities of the necessary flexibility and adaptability to meet the particular demands of the 1980s and 1990s.[1]

More specifically, critics—presumably from outside academia—imply that we in the academic community fail to monitor the performance of tenured faculty. Such allegations call into question whether we have addressed our responsibilities as assiduously as we have defended our privileges. In our own defense, we can all point to systems of faculty evaluation of various kinds that operate, in most cases, within the tenure system. We can also affirm, as Van Alstyne did so eloquently a decade ago, that tenure is not an invulnerable shield for every incompetency. On the other hand, we know that some of our tenured colleagues no longer meet their responsibilities. We suspect that while, de jure, tenure is not an invulnerable shield, de facto it is very nearly so on most campuses. This security is not simply a matter of administrative incompetence. The very condition that creates the need for the protections of academic freedom—a rapidly and unpredictably changing knowledge base—ensures that current tenure practices will shield all but the grossest misconduct.

Such widespread criticism of the tenure system makes those of us in the academic community nervous because we sense that the public does not fully understand or accept the rationale for tenure. The real source of our unease, however, is our fear that the public may never have fully understood or accepted the transformation of the modern university into an institution with a fundamental responsibility not only for training and research but for questioning all of society's current arrangements as well. In short, our concern is and ought to be whether the public understands the role and need for academic freedom itself.

Further, it is an appropriate moment to take up tenure issues not simply because of our critics' views but because the role of the university in society may be changing. Current notions of academic freedom and tenure arose in response to the new and expanded role of the modern university. If that role should again change significantly, academic freedom and tenure would have to be reevaluated.

In my view, the academic community need not be defensive about the tenure system, but we must be frank about its costs as well as its benefits. Members of the academic community enjoy a special balance of privileges and responsibilities, which is not a divine right but a recognition of our appropriate role in society. If we are to address the various contemporary pressures surrounding the privileges we enjoy and assess their future prospects, we must first increase our understanding of the history and rationale of the system itself and of the responsibilities it implies.[2] Only by putting the tenure system in this larger context can we continue to exert the necessary leadership on this issue.

Some History

When members of any successful profession, such as the professoriat, defend their current practices and privileges, they may be tempted to present them as the desirable, if not inevitable, heritage of ancient precedents. They may wish to portray their own prerogatives as emerging from an epic historical struggle and to insist that they serve the broader interests of society and posterity. So it is not surprising that contemporary college and university faculties— often joined by trustees and administrators—usually think of academic freedom and the corollary practice of academic tenure as the contemporary expression of an ancient right. The widespread currency of this notion, however incorrect, reflects the strong bond that many faculty members feel with those great thinkers of the past who strove to pursue the truth as they saw it, free from external harassment.

It is both interesting and troubling that so much mythology clings to the idea that academic freedom was bequeathed us by the universities of the Middle Ages. To be sure, when universities were small and insignificant, they were relatively independent bodies with certain privileges of self-governance. At times they were also centers of power and prestige, producing new and independent views on certain subjects. Overwhelmingly, however, they were institutions of great intellectual conformity—usually enforced from within but buttressed when necessary from without. The predominance of religious doctrine in universities virtually precluded free inquiry; intellectual freedom was not considered either necessary or appropriate for members of these communities. In fact, far from promoting open inquiry, the medieval university was instrumental in imposing orthodox views on other members of society.

Before the Civil War, American universities followed much the same pattern, although new elements in their institutional structure reflected the reality of American life in those times. From the beginning of American higher education, the trustees, not the faculty, constituted the college or university in the eyes of the law. As Hofstadter and Metzger point out, faculties were perceived as the obedient servants of the president, the trustees, and the community, whose views they were expected to uphold both inside and outside the classroom. Invested with the weighty responsibility of shaping their students' moral character, faculty members were expected not only to deliver the appropriate conventional pieties in the classroom but also to behave decorously in their public *and* private lives. Academic freedom as we know it was neither intended nor contemplated. Concerned mainly with preserving current knowledge and promoting morality, the faculties of these early American colleges would hardly be considered, either then or now, an independent group of scholars searching for new arrangements in science and society and exploring new systems of values.

In the late nineteenth century, however, faculty members at many German universities began to assume responsibility for developing new ideas in science and society and to expect the freedom of inquiry—at least within the university walls—associated with this ideal. As universities elsewhere began to follow the German model, the need for a setting congenial to inquiry and discovery led them to refine the idea of academic freedom. In the United States, this idea coincided with the establishment of public universities, which would take on an expanded set of functions and responsibilities.

Thus, at American universities, we have yet to celebrate the centennial of academic freedom and the particular institution that supports it, academic tenure. In the sweep of history these are very recent practices indeed, both here and abroad. Although independent thinkers have struggled since ancient times to free themselves from persecution for their ideas, the notion that universities require such freedom to play their assigned role properly did not emerge until the nineteenth century. In my judgment this concept of academic freedom as a defining ingredient of the modern university reflects the profoundly changed function of universities during the past century.

What precipitated this change was a radical shift in the underlying structure of belief. In the course of the nineteenth century a new belief in the redemptive power of intellectual discovery and insight, of reason and inquiry, began to replace the centuries-old trust in the redemptive power of religious faith. As in Tennyson's "Ulysses," humankind was urged "To follow knowledge like a sinking star / Beyond the utmost bounds of human thought." A new faith arose in the capacity of human beings to improve their condition through their own efforts and to achieve continual material, moral, and spiritual progress. The great engine of progress was thought to be undergirded by the "scientific attitude," which required its disciples to search for truth without prejudice, to analyze cause and effect, to distinguish fact from theory, and to form or discard opinions on the basis of evidence.

Universities came to be seen as providing the appropriate setting for such scientific as well as humanistic inquiry, which was increasingly regarded as a precondition for human progress. It is here that the chief justification for the system of academic tenure can be found: tenure was designed as the guarantor of academic freedom in that it allowed the objectivity and independence necessary to new understanding, which was itself necessary for human progress.

As inquiry began to take precedence over dogma on university campuses, the universities themselves were slowly transformed. This transformation required new arrangements between society and the universities and between the universities and their faculties. Should inquiry and change become less central to university-based education and scholarship and other values and objectives take priority, another transformation may be in order. Academic freedom may or may not be a critical component of such a future community.

Reflections on the Future of Academic Tenure

The contemporary notion of academic freedom is inextricably linked to society's attitudes toward progress and to the role of universities and faculties within such a context. To contemplate the future of academic freedom and tenure, we must first consider how effectively they are currently achieving their ends. We ought not to focus simply on procedural perfections of the well-worn set of practices that is currently in place.

We might approach this task by asking how effective tenure has been in helping to (1) protect the faculty from arbitrary and capricious personnel actions by trustees, administrators, or government officials; (2) stimulate a steady stream of new ideas and approaches within the academic community; (3) ensure that all college and university students are introduced to alternative visions of our present and future; and (4) establish an open campus environment in which alternative approaches are tolerated and evaluated with intellectual discipline.

With respect to preventing arbitrary personnel actions, tenure has clearly been very successful, but effectiveness in the other areas is more difficult to measure. The climate and accomplishments of higher education are influenced by many factors in addition to tenure. On balance, academic tenure seems to have had a beneficial effect in all four areas, yet I believe that U.S. faculties are presently falling short of their responsibilities at least with respect to the last two. The great bulk of our teaching remains uninformed by alternative approaches, intolerance of certain ideas is commonplace, and we do not always insist on an intellectually disciplined evaluation of new ideas.

Thus, although academic tenure has appropriately prevented certain ill-considered administrative acts, many faculty members have apparently failed to assume the full responsibility implied by its privilege. This situation is not, I would argue, likely to be remedied by a periodic evaluation of tenured faculty that is linked to tenure. Such an evaluation in itself is simply good personnel policy; it can enhance professional development and allow colleagues to assist one another, especially if it is both rigorous and constructive. But a "linked" evaluation—given that in the current environment tenure is scarcely ever revoked—would only generate paperwork without improving the tenure system.[3] Much more useful, in fact, is periodic evaluation of entire units, a practice common in most universities but little appreciated by the public.

Our first task as members of the higher education community is not periodic evaluation of tenured faculty members but an evaluation of the general teaching and research environment of the university. We must ensure the academic freedom of the college or university as a whole, as well as defending our prerogatives as individuals under the tenure system.

The due process procedures that now frame our understanding of tenure do not adequately address the many external and internal pressures to conform. What protects a particular faculty member against nonadministrative pressures to conform—some subtle, some less so, some within the university, some outside it? Such pressures come, for example, from the need to secure and retain grant funding from governmental and other agencies; from the attempt to shape projects to perceived institutional goals and values; from a desire for the approval of colleagues and peers; from public opinion; even from students. Not least among the internal pressures toward conformity, even toward a kind of orthodoxy, are the rapidly escalating demands of many students and faculty members that their institutions take official positions on various issues.

Sadly, faculties are often as guilty as the public in their intolerance for alternative ideas. Neither college administrators nor faculty bodies behaved admirably during the McCarthy era, and neither group now fully champions the notion that academic freedom should permeate the university community as a whole. Those scholars who first defined the nature and form of academic tenure in American universities understood that internal pressures could undermine the objectives of the system they were formulating. They relied on the professional ethics of the faculty to alleviate these pressures—a safeguard that has worked moderately well but not well enough. We must once again commit ourselves to attaining openness, objectivity, independence, and variety in the academic setting. If we should fail in this goal, academic freedom and tenure would simply become euphemisms for job security and the status quo instead of ensuring society an independent group of scholar-teachers. I do not mean to imply that because the current system is not perfect, we should abandon one of its essential elements— academic tenure. On the contrary, tenure should be strengthened through a heightened commitment to our joint responsibilities.

Academic freedom is, of course, never absolute. It is instead one of many values that must coexist in an increasingly complex world. Moreover, the phrase "academic freedom" suggests at once too much and too little. On the one hand, it proposes the possibility that teaching and research *can be* free of constraints. On the other hand, it fails to acknowledge the ever-present limits on those activities that result from other values we hold. Even a cursory glance at contemporary university life reveals limits on every side to the pursuit of teaching and research: restrictions of time and resources;

departmental and other obligations; the boundaries attributable to various canons of professional ethics, established procedures and paradigms, and federal government guidelines. Finally, there are the constraints imposed by the intellectual discipline of what we know as the scientific method.

But an even larger set of issues also needs to be addressed. Is tenure simply an artifact of the rise of the new science in the nineteenth century and the consequent change in the role of the university? Will tenure become unnecessary if society finds alternatives to the scientific method or devises other institutions (such as nonprofit "thinkers" and research laboratories) to share the current role of universities? Even now the scholarly community extends well beyond our campus walls. Scholars without the full benefits of academic freedom and tenure are developing important new insights in many areas. Interestingly, dismissal without due process (that is, some kind of hearing) is now less and less acceptable in many noneducational settings. With respect to the continued tenability of the scientific method, some analysts, even on university campuses, maintain that we have transcended the notion of scientific progress as an ideal and have started to find other guiding principles for forming our reality. Pure inquiry may give way to other values. Would such a turn of events bring us to abandon the concept of tenure? However we eventually answer these questions, society's continued commitment to progress, change, and the role of inquiry will determine both the future of tenure and the future of the university.

1. It is normally argued that the tenured faculty work assiduously to protect the academic freedom of the nontenured faculty and research staff. This is a slender reed indeed for our junior colleagues and our nontenured research staff who are major contributors to most college and university programs. It reflects a kind of paternalism that tenured faculties would, quite correctly, find unacceptable.

2. My understanding of the issues I will discuss is very much influenced by the classic works of R. Hofstadter and Walter P. Metzger.

3. For those institutions facing a mandated policy of "linked" post-tenure evaluations, we must develop, if possible, a system that will not completely undermine our notion of academic freedom.

Excellence and Equity

The word *excellence* is part of the daily rhetoric of academic life, yet it remains difficult to define. Though an ancient notion, excellence alludes to what is at once the most obvious and the most ineffable of human ideals. In all of its meanings, however, it represents a standard, perhaps transitory, against which our ideas, activities, and achievements can be judged.

In ancient Greek society education and excellence were closed related concepts. The very purpose of education was to nurture excellence—considered an essential aspect of life—and thus allow the fullest possible development of human potential. Unlike the Greeks, our society displays a certain ambivalence about accepting excellence as an ideal. Perhaps this ambivalence can be attributed to the growing body of critical thought in both science and letters that projects an aura of pessimism about the ultimate potentialities of the human experience. Some of us, on the other hand, still agree with C. Wright Mills, who concluded that "History is not yet done with its exploration of the limits or meanings of 'human nature.' " Like Mills, I continue to believe that there are human possibilities we have not yet dreamed of.

In recent years, the ambivalence of our society toward the ideal of excellence has been especially marked in relation to intellectual achievement, thus cutting at the very heart of higher education. Today, for whatever reason, we often waver in our commitment to excellence in intellectual achievement and wonder whether and in what circumstances we should seek it in ourselves, our peers, and some of our social institutions. Ironically, we suffer no such uncertainty in the areas of industrial and agricultural production, consumer goods, or the performing arts. Perhaps this vacillation stems from the acknowledged power, for good *and* ill, vested in the achievement of intellectual excellence and in the simultaneous recognition that excellence is not an egalitarian concept.

Our society has always experienced a healthy tension between the ideas of egalitarianism and the desire to acknowledge individual achievement. The two principles, egalitarianism and individual achievement, have always represented competing models for distributing national resources and other forms of recognition and power. But the continued existence of inequalities and inequities in our society, along with the rapid expansion of our knowledge base, may make some people suspicious of superior intellectual accomplishment. In some ways this skepticism is understandable, for our rapidly expanding knowledge will tend to increase the relative power and rewards derived from intellectual accomplishment unless we simultaneously devote more attention and resources to educational opportunity. As with other types of social change, swiftly changing technology and knowledge can create uncertainty, ambivalence, and social tension. We must, therefore, match our investments in creating new knowledge with investments that will help us share access to such knowledge. Any other policy would undermine our efforts to achieve social justice and should not be tolerated.

Within the context of this ambivalence toward intellectual achievement, institutions that are unequivocally dedicated to the goal of excellence in teaching and research sometimes draw accusations of elitism. Some critics suggest that it is inappropriate for any institution of higher education to strive for excellence, thereby distinguishing itself from others. Such views reflect a profound misunderstanding of both the role of the modern university and the necessary diversity of educational institutions in our society. Moreover, if these views gain currency, they may frustrate some of society's best opportunities to improve the human condition.

Since the late nineteenth century the role of U.S. universities has been to provide a suitable setting for free scientific and humanistic inquiry. At least two critical attributes of modern universities result from this role. First, the work of universities often challenges the status quo—whether in science or other areas—thereby creating a natural tension between universities and the societies that support them. This tension may account for some of the suspicion of excellence coming from outside academia. Second, the pursuit of excellence, or the attempt to push forward the frontiers of knowledge as far as creativity will allow, is an absolutely necessary aspect of the way universities meet their responsibilities to society as a whole.

These responsibilities rest most especially on those universities that have acquired the human and physical resources necessary to contribute significantly to our knowledge base and that have demonstrated the ability to use these resources wisely. Such institutions have a special obligation to press their capacities and those of their students to the utmost. In this context, the pursuit of excellence in research, in teaching, and in service is more than merely a legitimate aspiration for institutions of higher education; it becomes a critical part of the dynamic by which such institutions fulfill their social role.

In our continual search for excellence in all aspects of university life, we must constantly reevaluate all of our academic programs. Since teaching comprises the most important single function of our colleges and universities, let us dwell for a moment on reevaluating our efforts toward excellence in teaching. I believe we too seldom ask ourselves what constitutes excellent teaching and how excellence in teaching can best be encouraged within the context of the societal function of universities. What we need to know is whether our teaching programs contribute significantly to students' abilities to realize their potential as creative individuals, as thoughtful citizens, as professionals, and as scholars. Do our programs produce students who can communicate clearly, reason and make critical judgments, distinguish facts from values, understand our cultural and artistic heritage? Excellent teaching programs should produce students with all these skills in addition to a portfolio of important professional tools and knowledge.

Unfortunately, teaching programs in higher education are often structured with an overwhelming specialty focus. Individual departments control curriculum design, with college or university curriculum committees exercising only a marginal influence. Our challenge is to allow continued departmental autonomy without abandoning our students to various scholarly ghettos. How, for example, do we prevent the undergraduate major from becoming merely the preparation for a graduate degree in a particular field?

To monitor the quality of teaching, we must constantly review the teaching environment in our colleges and universities. Class size, teaching load, class structure, course content and/or teaching methods, availability of library materials or instructional equipment must all be frequently reassessed. Each teaching program will need to address somewhat different problems, but perhaps conversations on this topic could be stimulated by some of these questions:

- What constitutes excellence in teaching and what type of resources, personal and institutional, enhance such excellence?
- Is our goal to educate students for their own satisfaction? For present social needs? For future social needs? What does each of these goals imply about the desirable characteristics for our instructional programs?
- Could existing educational resources, such as class scheduling, academic advising, and support services, be more effective than they are now?
- How can enthusiasm for teaching remain an important element in every faculty member's commitment to the university?

We must find ways, even in difficult times, of continually infusing fresh vitality into the enterprise of teaching. We must aspire to new levels of excellence in this crucial aspect of our academic mission, just as we do in our research and scholarly activities.

Moreover, our measures of excellence will need to change to suit the exigencies of a changing world. The United States participates in a worldwide economic, social, and political structure whose members are becoming increasingly interdependent. Our lives are constantly affected by ideas and products that have been developed elsewhere, just as we ourselves export our new ideas and products to an ever larger set of nations. In such an environment, public policy and private initiatives must nourish those efforts and institutions that enable us to import and export the best new ideas and products, regardless of where they are developed or where they are needed. We can only meet our collective responsibilities by maintaining institutions, public and private, profit and nonprofit, that can hold themselves to a national and international standard of excellence. Thus the pursuit of excellence has now become both more challenging and more necessary.

At the same time, we must recognize that these accelerating standards for excellence merely reinforce the need for increased attention to issues of equity. Some critics argue that striving for intellectual excellence actually militates against equality and social justice, which are central goals of a democratic society. To be sure, the relationships among justice, equality, freedom of choice, and excellence are complex, and we have yet to discover the joint optima of commitment to each of these objectives. I continue to believe, however, that a commitment to excellence, within the context of a concern for all members of society, remains the most viable framework for seeking our various social objectives.

In fact, we often forget that one of the few standards of performance that helps sustain a democracy is actual achievement. In my view, rewards for achievement are morally justified and can serve as a crucial guarantee against the autocracy of birth, wealth, and other vested interests. The result of gauging achievement by a standard of excellence can be a society that puts all human abilities to their maximum and best use.

We should also remember that one important aim of our educational system is to remove obstacles from the paths of individuals so that their natural abilities can flourish. An educational system which includes institutions that hold themselves to the highest standards in teaching and research should function as a pathway for all those with the necessary ability. This obligation raises the whole question of affirmative action in hiring and admissions.

Historically, the concept of affirmative action was preceded by the broader and more basic notion of nondiscrimination. The Civil Rights Act of 1964 was the first in a long series of laws addressing this issue. In 1965 the first Executive Order applicable to government contractors mandated not only nondiscrimination but affirmative action. In more recent years, many of the basic concepts underlying affirmative action programs have survived significant constitutional challenge. When one of the first test cases in this arena came before the Supreme Court, the justices described the legitimate purpose of affirmative action programs as "the removal of built-in headwinds" that hinder underrepresented groups from being judged on the basis of their individual merits.

In a university setting, affirmative action is a commitment to a process, a set of procedures, a method of decision making intended to remove these built-in headwinds so that underrepresented populations can become more fully competitive in the academic world. It is important to understand that affirmative action measures, when properly applied, do not mandate preferential hiring or admissions and need not subvert a university's commitment to excellence. Rather, by ensuring nondiscrimination, such measures should buttress long-term efforts to achieve distinction in teaching and research. Excellence and equity can and should be mutually supportive goals.

It is, however, necessary to sound a cautionary note about the length and difficulty of the road leading to equality. Let us not deceive ourselves that centuries of discrimination will be easily overturned. Indeed, despite the expenditure of considerable effort and resources, most colleges and universities have fallen short of their objectives in attracting underrepresented populations. There is, for example, disturbing news that the enrollment of Black students in our nation's undergraduate and graduate programs is declining. We need renewed commitment, additional resources, and fresh ideas if we are to realize our affirmative action goals.

In order to play the fullest possible part in individual and social development, education must be open to everyone with the necessary aptitude and motivation, but it must also nurture unusual talents and abilities. In particular, we must not hold ourselves aloof from the hopes of those in our society who are, for a variety of academically irrelevant reasons, underrepresented in our student bodies, or on our faculties and staffs. We have a shared but direct responsibility to help ensure the fullest possible development of all members of our society who wish to participate in the pursuit of our academic goals. Only by remedying underrepresentation can our colleges and universities meet their obligation to cultivate the intellectual, aesthetic, and economic potential of society. These efforts should not be separate from but integral to our pursuit of excellence.

Thus, in my opinion, questions about the legitimacy of excellence as an individual and institutional aspiration yield to the realization of its social necessity. Excellence, always tempered by equity, functions not to challenge but to complement and support the myriad other aims of our society.